Nov. 19, 2009

MERGERS

BY STEVEN L. LAYNE

J
LAY

PELICAN PUBLISHING COMPANY
GRETNA 2006

Library of Congress Cataloging-in-Publication Data

Layne, Steven L.
  Mergers / Steven L. Layne.
    p. cm.
  Summary: Four "deviant" teenagers, each with a special power,
struggle to survive in a future where the Legion for World
Alliance has merged all the earth's peoples into one combined
race.
  ISBN-13: 978-1-58980-183-7 (hardcover : alk. paper)
  [1. Science fiction.]   I. Title.
  PZ7.L44675Me 2006
  [Fic]—dc22
                                                2005032652

Jacket art by Nathan R. Baron

Printed in the United States of America

Published by Pelican Publishing Company, Inc.
1000 Burmaster Street, Gretna, Louisiana 70053

To *Pamela Albers*
for staying up late and opening new doors,
and
to *Debby Krueger-Hipes*
for giving a guy a chance.

ACKNOWLEDGMENTS

Each book is its own journey, and this one has been interesting indeed. As has been my custom, I have involved teachers, librarians, and students from schools all over the country throughout the many drafts of this book. Without them, the effort would be in vain; I am eternally grateful to them. They include the 2004-2005 classes of:

Dr. Karen Biggs-Tucker from Wildrose Elementary School in St. Charles, IL—Grade 5; Mrs. Gail Boushey from Meridian Elementary School in Kent, WA—Grades 5/6; Mrs. Val Cawley, Mr. Eric Chisausky, Ms. Melissa Zaniewski, and Mrs. Anna Lee from Butler Junior High School in Oak Brook, IL—Grade 7; Dr. Jill Cole from Wesley College in Dover, DE—undergraduates; Mrs. Christine Moen from Dakota Junior/Senior High School in Dakota, IL—Grade 8; Mrs. Tammy Potts from Gower Middle School in Burr Ridge, IL—Grade 8; Mrs. Peggy Short from Skyview Middle School in Colorado Springs, CO—Grade 8; and Mrs. Tonya Wilt from Jackson Middle School in Jackson, OH—Grade 8.

Serving in an advisory capacity in the areas of biology, chemistry, and neuroscience were Dr. Elizabeth Juergensmeyer, Dr. Rolf Myhrman, and Dr. Richard Newkirk—professors at Judson College in Elgin, IL. I so appreciate the generous sharing of their expertise.

To my faithful panel of pre-publication readers and critics—is it possible to write a book without people like you? Not for me. Special recognition to Pam Albers, Kathy

Dickson, Debby Krueger-Hipes, Joan Moser, Susan Roberts, Joy Towner, and Susan Wilke for caring enough to tell the truth and doing all that was asked of them.

Love to my wife, Debbie, for traveling the road with me, and to Grayson, Victoria, and Jackson for freeing me up now and then to write. Thanks to our Heavenly Father for His faithfulness in seeing this book through from start to finish.

MERGERS

MERGERS
MAIN CHARACTERS

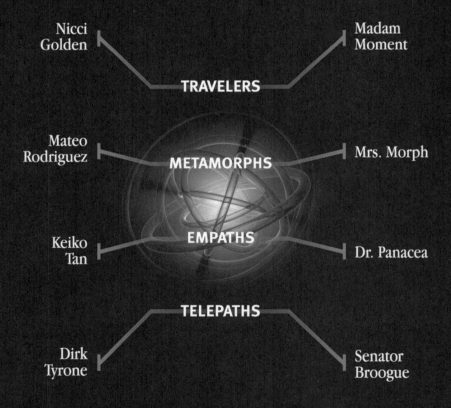

Nicci Golden

Madam Moment

TRAVELERS

Mateo Rodriguez

METAMORPHS

Mrs. Morph

EMPATHS

Keiko Tan

Dr. Panacea

TELEPATHS

Dirk Tyrone

Senator Broogue

irk Tyrone shifted uneasily. He was groggy. His mind, usually so alert and powerful, seemed incapable of clear thought. He moved to raise his hands to his temples, a habit that typically brought his extraordinary mental powers into focus, but was unsuccessful. His arms were pinned to the wall on either side of him by what felt like some type of metal braces. His legs were secured in a similar fashion, and there seemed to be a shield over the top half of his face. Dirk opened his eyes to the blackness of the shield and felt a pulsating energy running through it. His muddled thoughts continued. Why was it so difficult to concentrate? Then, he felt the shield vibrate; a surge of power erupted from within it when he tried to focus his thoughts. Whoever had captured him clearly knew how to keep him from using his powers, or so they thought.

Without warning, a scream of agony echoed from all around him. The source was female. If he had Keiko's abilities, he could remove the woman's pain almost instantaneously—drawing it into himself and then dispelling it from his body at a slow but steady pace—but that was Keiko's power, not his. No, the way he could best help this woman would be to enter her mind and let her know that she was not alone. Either that or mentally attack whoever was hurting her. Another cry—and this one shook the very wall to which Dirk was shackled. It spoke of a physical pain so intense that he could not imagine it would be possible for the woman to survive much longer. Instinctively, Dirk's incredible mind attempted to leave his body and move in the direction of hers, but the shield immediately began to hum with energy in an effort to block his power. Dirk tensed. Something that felt like an enormous needle was slowly advancing toward the center of his mind.

"*This is not really happening,*" he told himself. "*This thing . . . this shield is just trying to distract me because it knows . . . Aaaahhh!*" The needle lanced through some soft spongy matter in his brain, and he fought down a growing sense of panic. "*That didn't really happen. I'm supposed to think it happened, but it didn't.*" Someone was playing mental games with him, but whoever it was didn't understand Dirk's sense of self-preservation. He gritted his teeth, created an image in his mind of the shield blasting into a million pieces, and then played it over and over again like a tune that just wouldn't go away. As if in response, the hum of the shield became a strong buzz, and the needle retaliated as if it were a living being under attack—jabbing out viciously at Dirk's brain in every direction. Sweat streamed down the sides of his face sending salty streams to his lips as the image he was creating in his mind intensified. Now, the energy around the shield was crackling ferociously, and water was collecting inside Dirk's eyes. "*Somebody's . . . uhhh . . . gonna win this . . . fight . . . and it's not . . . uhhh . . . gonna be YOU!*"

Sparks sprayed the air, and the device exploded, filling the dimly lit chamber with bright light for a brief moment. Dirk had won! Now that the shield was gone, he could take in his surroundings visually and use his powers without difficulty. Still, he was anchored to the wall, and he could see that the bonds holding him were sturdy.

A high-pitched scream was followed by another cry of anguish. This one, though, was weaker. In his battle against the shield, Dirk had nearly forgotten about the woman. She was clearly dying and although he could not physically break free and go to her, his mind was capable of movement outside of his body. Mentally, he raced through the halls of the complex. This place was unfamiliar to him. He took a wrong turn that led him to a dead end. He backtracked and headed off down another hallway still trying to shake off the aftereffect of the shield and clear his mind.

He never ceased to be somewhat in awe of his powers. His physical body was back there, bound to a wall, incapable of movement, and yet mentally he was here, in these hallways, searching desperately for someone he did not even know. He rounded a corner and halted. She was just ahead. He approached cautiously, knowing that if he entered her mind too rapidly he might frighten her. Still, he could not afford to be as gentle as he would have liked; her psyche was crumbling. If he did not act now, it would be too late.

As gingerly as he could, Dirk entered her mind. *"I'm here."* He spoke softly. *"You are not alone. I'm not going to hurt you."* His way was blocked. A wall had appeared—typical—the mind's involuntary first defense against psychic intrusion. The woman could remove it easily if she chose, but she was frightened and in intense pain. Dirk's formidable psychic ability could easily break it down, but in her fragile state it might further harm her. It would be safer if he could talk her into removing it. *"I'm a friend who's come to help you. My name is Dirk . . ."*

"Dirk!" The woman seemed to recognize his name, and as she gasped it aloud the tone in her voice was startlingly familiar. Instantly, the wall faded away, and their minds merged. The result was a cry of desperation from both Dirk's mental and physical selves, for as he sought to comfort this woman in what was likely the hour of her death, he recognized her.

Dr. Lisa Tyrone—once a celebrated geneticist of the Legion for World Alliance—had been labeled a dangerous criminal only days after Dirk's birth. Her disappearance from a hospital with four newborns had led to the largest manhunt in world history. The general population had no idea why this woman was being sought—only that the reward for information leading to her capture was tremendous. The average housewives and businessmen, school teachers and firemen did not know that one of the babies she had taken was her own nephew, Dirk Tyrone, and that the parents of all four infants had been murdered within moments of the children's births. The police and government investigators did not know that Dr. Tyrone and these babies held a secret that could bring the world's leaders to their knees. They would stop at nothing to silence her. She had managed to evade capture for many years as she raised Dirk and the other infants in hiding, but their luck had finally run out two days ago when their shelter was stormed by Alliance guards.

"Aunt Lisa!" Dirk's mind was now joined with his aunt's, and her nearness to death filled him with dread. *"Save your strength, Aunt Lisa. Don't speak—just answer in your mind. Do you know if the others have been captured?"*

Lisa Tyrone's mind formed a response in a slow and halting manner. *"Matty . . . escaped . . . they wa . . . want . . . wanted me . . . to . . . to tell them . . . where he . . . uhhhh!"* Her mind moved to an unconscious state without warning, and Dirk was left, mentally, alone. Uncertainty began to gnaw at his insides. Despite all of Dirk's mental abilities, it had been Lisa Tyrone's mind that had always been confident and decisive. Her decisions had kept them safe all these years. She had told Dirk many times that he was a born leader, but he had never felt like one. And at this precise moment, he was reminded of how inept a leader he would make. His aunt was dying, and if he thought about that—truly accepted it— he knew he would give up. Let the Alliance do what they wanted with him. Wouldn't it be easier? Anything would be easier than having to make a decision right now. What should he do? He felt the need to take action, but he did not know what action he should take. *"They'd drum me out of the leadership brigade real quick,"* he chided himself.

His thoughts turned to his three friends—none of whom he had seen since he had been taken prisoner. *"So Matty's on the loose—score one for our side,"* he thought. Mateo Rodriguez, affectionately known as Matty to his friends, would prove difficult for the Alliance to catch because of his incredible transformational ability. Mateo could literally alter his form to become any living creature—real or imagined. Although the Alliance guards didn't know about Mateo's ability, Dirk figured his friend would reveal his power to them if it would keep him from captivity.

When the guards raided their shelter, Dirk had quickly lost track of everyone. He remembered, though, that Matty had not been inside when they appeared. The Alliance had clearly been torturing Lisa Tyrone—most likely trying to force her to give them some piece of useful information that would help them find the boy. Of course, his aunt had not said a word to endanger Matty. They were fools to think she would. She had raised Dirk, Mateo, and the girls from birth to their fifteenth year. Having no parents, and with the need to keep their very existence a secret, she was the only mother any of them had ever known. What kind of mother would betray one of her children?

Keiko Tan tried to calm herself as she paced the floor of the small room in which she had been imprisoned. She had not eaten in several hours, but far worse than the lack of nourishment was the lack of social interaction. Keiko *needed* people. She needed them in a way that set her apart from others. She surveyed herself in the reflection of the shiny black surface of the walls. Her dark almond-shaped eyes were beginning to cloud over, and the warm olive skin tone that typified her Asian heritage was growing pallid—the result of captivity.

Where was Dirk? And why had he not contacted her? The two of them shared a unique psychic link that Dirk had put in place one afternoon when he confessed that he wanted them to be "more than friends." That had been nearly a year ago, and since that time, a sense of his mental presence had always been with her . . . until now. The idea that Dirk might be in pain—the thought of any of her friends being physically harmed—served only to further weaken her, but she could not seem to discipline her mind away from such thoughts. She longed for Dirk's mental gifts right now—for her own were doing her no good. She was an *empath,* a healer. Physical contact with other living creatures both strengthened her and provided her the opportunity to use her power to cure the slightest physical ailment or to soothe a troubled spirit. Keiko Tan's captors were shrewd, she'd give them that. By isolating her, they were not only preventing her from using her remarkable empathic powers to help the other prisoners, but they were also achieving their primary goal—her death. For just as Keiko infused energy and healing into others in their time of need, it was their lifeforce, the living energy of other beings, which somehow seemed to provide for her own continued existence. Here, in this tiny black room, it seemed that her worst fear had been given a life of its own. She was going to suffocate from loneliness and die, separated from any other sign of life.

Mateo Rodriguez had assumed the appearance of an Alliance guard with ease—but maintaining it was proving difficult. Twice, he had felt the shape of his physical body beginning to return to its true form when guards appeared unexpectedly in the halls of the complex. He had stabilized his transformation quickly, but if anyone had been looking directly *into* his eyes, they would have seen a tiny image in his pupils—a picture, in essence, of the guard whose shape he had assumed. While he'd had plenty of chances to practice his power of transformation in the shelter where he and his friends had been raised by Lisa Tyrone, there had rarely been a need to *maintain* a shape in a dangerous situation like this. When Mateo got nervous, he tended to return to his true form—that of a Hispanic teenage boy—the *only* Hispanic teenage boy in the world as far as he knew. And right now, every guard in the Alliance was looking for him. If he did not gain control over his appearance, he would endanger himself and the friends he was here to rescue.

The metal cell door opened quickly as he slid his key into the slot outside. The body of his friend Nicci Golden lay on a solid slab of granite. Her chest did not appear to rise or fall as he crossed the cell. He assumed she had been drugged, but perhaps they had killed her. After all, that was what they were going to do eventually—right? That's what they were going to do to all of them—destroy them because they were different—because they didn't *look* like the other people walking the streets of cities all over their world. The Legion for World Alliance made no exceptions, and if there was anything Lisa Tyrone had instilled in the teens, it was that they were, indeed, exceptions. What she couldn't explain . . . or *wouldn't* explain . . . was why it mattered so much.

In quiet moments, Lisa Tyrone had often told herself that the four young people she had raised and protected since birth belonged in an earlier time—a time when words like *ancestry* and *heritage* were terms that held meaning to people. Now, those days were gone and, sadly, most of the people walking the planet today had no knowledge that such terms had ever existed. In the engineered society developed by the Alliance, her nephew and his friends could never successfully integrate. So they had been hunted like animals, and she had kept them safe. To the leaders of the Alliance, Mateo, Dirk, Keiko, and Nicci were nothing more than remnants of a time when the Earth had more than one race—a time before the Merger.

CHAPTER 2

Mateo took Nicci's limp wrist in his hand and felt for a pulse. Yes! She was alive. As he looked at her lying there, her lovely dark skin as black as midnight, he was reminded of a tale he'd once heard of a sleeping princess who was awakened by a kiss. He grinned—tempted to try it—but then thought better of it. He'd tried to kiss Nicci once before—when they'd been out walking on a moonlit night. She'd been talking about the constellations as they gazed up at the stars, and her warm, deep voice had seemed almost hypnotic. Mateo remembered the scent of honeysuckle in the air and the soft breeze that had seemed to envelop him. He'd reached out to draw her near, and just as their lips were about to meet . . . her right fist made contact with his jaw.

He heard a slight groan now, and she stirred. This definitely ruled out the kiss. The last thing he needed was to explain another dislocated jaw to Dirk. Mateo watched as she blinked several times. Her eyes, a deep chestnut, widened as they fixed upon him, and her grogginess caused her to shrink back clumsily in fear. "Nicci, it's me," he said softly. "I came to get you out of here." She regarded the young man who appeared to be a security officer with suspicion, but suddenly the pupils of his eyes began to dilate and in them she saw the image of Mateo Rodriguez grinning out at her. Then, just as his eyes had foreshadowed, the physical being of the officer morphed into the brazen young man who had come to her rescue; Mateo was now standing before her.

"Matty! Are you ever a sight for sore eyes!" She stood and threw her arms around him in an embrace that lasted longer than she intended, for as she started to release him, her knees gave way. He caught her.

"Whoa there, Nicci! Not so fast. Whatever kinda juice they've been pumping into you, I don't think it's intended to build stamina." He helped her take a seat on the slab again. "Just give yourself a minute to come out of the fog, and then we'll get out of this joint."

"I'm not alone, Matty," she said gravely. "They have Dirk and Keiko, too . . . and Lisa." The horror in his eyes registered immediately. Once upon a time, Dr. Lisa Tyrone had been an incredibly powerful individual in the Alliance. In fact, she was one of a very select group who possessed any knowledge of world history prior to the Alliance's formation. She was also the one who had saved Mateo and his friends from destruction soon after their births. Though she had kept most of the details hidden from them, the teens all knew she had been their savior from the very beginning.

As one of the Alliance's leading geneticists, Dr. Tyrone had used her influence, which had been considerable at the time, to lobby for the chance to successfully "correct" the only four babies in the history of the Alliance who were not born with all racial characteristics blended or *merged*. Although their parents had been destroyed immediately to prevent any chance of future "problematic" births, the babies were given a reprieve at Dr. Tyrone's request. They were placed in an isolated wing of the hospital under her personal care. She had been given no nurses or attendants to assist her for fear that the fragile truth protected from all but the highest-ranking leaders of the Alliance would be revealed. She was given three days, though she begged for more, to merge the infants, and so she had begun work immediately.

There had been no sleep, no meals, no showers or conversations. There had been nothing but one woman, striving with all of the knowledge and physical stamina she possessed, to save four innocent newborns—who no longer had parents waiting to bring them home. She could not even take the time to grieve—for one of the infants belonged to her brother and sister-in-law. The best she could do to remember them was to keep their little boy, her nephew Dirk, alive. For three long days and nights, a remote ward of the hospital had echoed with no sound but the cries of four tiny infants and a lone voice asking questions whose answers proved evasive. And while Dr. Lisa Tyrone used every tool and God-given gift at her disposal to preserve life, the Alliance moved stealthily into her home and murdered her husband.

"Nicci!" Mateo pulled her quickly to her feet. "Do you know what they'll *do* to her?" The panic in his voice sent shivers down her spine. He grabbed her arms with a ferocious intensity, and it was clear that all concern for her fatigued state was set aside. "Nichelle, we have to go to her, now!"

She blinked at his use of her full name, and though Lisa Tyrone had told her that the name *Nichelle* was chosen quite purposefully, the shortened *Nicci* had become habit—except when she was in trouble. "I don't know if I can, Mateo!" He knew what he was asking, but he had no idea what it would take from within her to accomplish the task—especially in her weakened condition. One look at his intense gaze told her that he probably didn't care.

"Nicci, you have to try. We may already be too late."

"I can't take us both, Mateo, I'm too weak."

He stared at her and made no reply.

"I *won't* take you with me. You'll have to find your own way." Her voice was filled with reluctance as usual. Nicci's ability to travel through time was nothing more than a curse in her eyes, and she was less practiced in the use of her power because she avoided any situation that invited her to demonstrate it. The others joked, but with an undercurrent of seriousness, that Nicci had so many *conditions*—

conditions that had to be met before she would use her ability—that *time* quite literally marched on without her. For example, she always moved into the future and never into the past—not because she *couldn't* but because she *wouldn't*. "It's much more complicated to go backward," she insisted although she had never, to anyone's knowledge, tried moving into the past before. Also, she *very* rarely moved another person with her through time. "It takes too much out of me," she told the others. "You wouldn't understand, but trust me when I tell you, it's painful traveling with a passenger."

She knew Matty expected her to give in at the last minute and take him with her, but he was in for a surprise. Whatever they had done to her in this facility had not only knocked her out but had also drained her of energy. She was, for the first time in her life, truly afraid she might not be able to control her own journey through time. To try to bring Mateo with her would have been the end for both of them.

Mateo's hands gestured with impatience. "Okay, you win. I'll find my own way. So go! GO!"

Nicci Golden took a deep breath and closed her eyes—concentrating on Lisa Tyrone—her teacher, surrogate mother, and friend. Mateo stood back, marveling as he always did, as a golden aura surrounded his friend. In an instant, she was gone—moving only the smallest fraction of a second into the future—to a moment in time that held the woman who had fought to save Nicci's life from the moment of her birth.

Moments later, as Mateo resumed the appearance of the Alliance security officer, an alarm sounded. Almost at once, and entirely against his will, Mateo reverted to the young Hispanic body that was truly his own. While Mateo could take the form of living creatures for indefinite periods of time, he could only assume the form of another human being for a short while. In addition, maintaining a human form other than his own took a great deal of concentration, and when Mateo became anxious his stability frequently faltered, causing him to revert to his true appearance. The tread of booted feet made its way quickly in his direction. Almost involuntarily the image of a wasp filled Mateo's pupils; he was airborne just as the guards came rushing into the hall.

As Nicci materialized a few feet from her target, she was bombarded by her own senses. Her nostrils flared at the smell of the burnt flesh that assaulted the air all around her. Her eyes moistened as she reached Lisa Tyrone's body, but the sound of a shrill alarm cut into the air, distracting her momentarily and slicing into her eardrums with a vengeance. "Matty," she thought. "They know I've escaped, or they know he's here—or both." She ignored the alarm as best she could and began looking for signs of life from Lisa. The woman was bolted to a rectangular table made from some type of metal that Nicci could not identify. The table itself was positioned on a raised platform in the center of a windowless room. Nicci shuddered at the sight before her.

Lisa Tyrone's mulatto skin, identical in color and texture to the skin of every other member of society—with the exception of Nicci and her friends—was now charred and blackened. "They torched you." Nicci said the words aloud and wished with every fiber of being they were untrue.

Torching was the name given to the Alliance's best-known method of punishment or information extraction—depending upon the circumstances. Prisoners were bolted to a surface that was charged from beneath its base with infrared heat. It was not unlike lying inside a massive frying pan with a healthy flame beneath it. And the Alliance had become most adept at using the device—a fact that received a great deal of press as it served to significantly curb illegal activity throughout the world. In fact, it had proven so successful that it was nearly always under study for improvements and modifications. The latest model allowed the surface to be heated in separate sections and in varying degrees as opposed to all at once, thereby slowing the torching process and providing multiple opportunities for prisoners to experience punishment or, as in the case of Dr. Tyrone, reveal information the Alliance was seeking. It was unnecessary to have guards around a prisoner during torching. The design of the device precluded any possibility of escape, and the offensive odor produced by the process was an annoyance to the Alliance Security Force.

Nicci saw Lisa's eyes flicker for a moment and then close again rapidly. She appeared to be taking very shallow breaths, but they were somewhat regular. No noise was coming from the machine itself, so Nicci assumed the torching was over. The *real* question—was it finished for the moment or for good? Carefully, she reached out to touch Lisa's hand, afraid of harming her skin which, if it had any nerve endings left, must feel as though it was on fire. The alarm continued to pulsate throughout the complex, yet interestingly no one had approached this area. As Nicci gingerly brushed Lisa's hand, another mind came hurtling into hers like a derailed locomotive. It was Dirk.

"Nicci! Nicci, she's dying!"

"Dirk? Where are you?" She knew that there was no need to verbalize anything. He could read her thoughts before she could form the words on her lips.

"I don't know. They have me chained up somewhere. They put a shield over my face to block my power, but I broke through. Nicci, Keiko's got to be here somewhere! We have to find her—you have to bring her to Aunt Lisa—before it's too late. I'm barely able to hold her conscious mind together. I can't do it much longer."

She avoided his request. *"Dirk, the alarms—they probably know that I'm free. Matty's here—they're after him, too. There isn't time to . . ."*

"You WILL do this, Nicci." He seized her mind—a psychic attack of the most violent nature. He took it from her with

no concern for her privacy or for her will. It was something he'd never imagined doing to a friend, but his aunt, their *"mother,"* was dying, and now he had an idea at least of how to save her. The fact that he suddenly, miraculously, had a plan meant that it had to be followed—right? Why should he waste time having a heart-to-heart discussion with Nicci when he had the power to simply make things happen? Keiko Tan was the only one who might be able to save his aunt, and since *he* couldn't bring Keiko to his aunt, *Nicci* was going to do it for him. His powerful mind forced her to call forth her ability, and he simultaneously reached out for Keiko—making use of the psychic link he had formed between them. With the shield gone, it was child's play to find her, but controlling Nicci's will at the same time was proving difficult.

"Keiko . . . are you . . ."

"I'm here, Dirk! Here!" Her response was so sudden that it surprised him. So she had been waiting for him to contact her! That was a *very* pleasant thought. Amazingly, his plan was working, too. Within an instant Nicci's body appeared in Keiko's tiny black prison, and Keiko felt the first surge of energy and adrenaline she had experienced in days. The sight of another person, let alone a good friend, was like food to a starving beggar. Meanwhile, Dirk sensed Keiko's weakness, and he poured his mental energies into her with reckless abandon. All at once, she seemed to be standing in an auditorium and everywhere around her there were people. They were smiling and cheering, and their hearts were full of gratitude and love for all the blessings of life.

Though the scene was a telepathic projection from Dirk's mind to hers, its effect was tremendous. Keiko radiated; she glowed in the presence of the crowd! None of it was real, but she experienced it as though it were, and the sickly pallor that had overtaken her was driven away from her body. Her lovely eyes became clear again. Dirk had given her nearly everything he had to give. She now would have the power, he hoped, to save his aunt, but he did *not* have the energy left to force Nicci to travel the distance back or to take a passenger with her. As his aura began to fade from Keiko's mind, he imparted the details of the past few moments into her consciousness. And then, he was gone. Keiko felt the pang of emptiness that always accompanied Dirk's leaving, but there was no time to dwell on their relationship right now. Lisa Tyrone's needs were immediate.

Nicci watched, knowingly, as Keiko's strength returned. She was angry at Dirk for pushing his will upon her, but she also understood. She knew that if he had not done so, she might not have been able to make the decision quickly enough. Keiko was eyeing her now, expecting even more than Dirk. She knew that Keiko needed her to take them both back to Lisa, but Nicci didn't think she could do it. Whenever she moved through time, she felt as if a small part of her that could never be recovered was left elsewhere. And for her to move through time repeatedly, without proper rest in between, was extremely painful. It was something she had never been able to explain to the others. At times, in the heat of an argument, she had been called selfish by Dirk, and Mateo had once accused her of "lacking heart." The sting of Mateo's comment resurrected itself for a moment, and she found herself lost in the memory of the circumstances that had led him to speak so harshly to her.

They had been enjoying one of their few days outside of the protected underground shelter where they lived in constant fear of being discovered by the Alliance. Every few weeks, Lisa allowed them a few hours outside in a heavily forested area nearby. It became known as "the picnic spot." It was during one of these outings that the four of them had found a puppy that appeared to have been shot and left for dead. It was not unusual for the Alliance Security Force to use animals, even domestic ones, for target practice. The nearest clinic was several miles away, and Keiko, much to her dismay, had never successfully healed a member of the animal kingdom. So it had fallen on Nicci to decide whether the puppy lived or died. Of course she had saved it. But she had hesitated for a moment before deciding to transport the dog to the doorstep of a clinic in town, and her hesitation was judged harshly by her male friends—particulary Matty, who was the group's resident animal lover. Keiko, though, had remained silent as Nicci weighed her decision to help the pup. Never judging, never questioning—that was Keiko, and somehow it was Keiko that Nicci did not want to disappoint now.

"Keiko, listen to me." Nicci tried to keep her voice from trembling. "I'm going to send you to Lisa without me. Come here."

The lithe Asian girl smiled warmly at her friend. She seemed always to know the truth even when it was not spoken. "Nicci, you're frightened. I understand your fear, but to remain here alone will not be any safer for you than traveling with me."

"But I can't travel with a companion. I just can't do it, Keiko. I've already transported twice today, and we're not out of here yet. Besides, they filled my arteries with some kind of drug, and I'm not sure the effect has totally worn off." Nicci's eyes pleaded for her friend's forgiveness as did the tone of her words.

"Nicci, we need to move fast. I don't want to argue, but I think we *must* stay together." Keiko had heard the alarm sound, and as it continued to resonate, her fears were mounting. "I will help you to do this. I *know* that it may hurt you. You will share your pain with me, and we will do it together." She grasped her friend's hands for a moment and, at her touch, Nicci's fears began to dissolve. For a brief moment, Keiko gasped as the true fullness of Nicci's fear was transferred into her empathic body. She experienced it, felt fear—Nicci's fear—just the way that Nicci had felt it. It alarmed her, but it did not overwhelm her. And after a few seconds had passed, Keiko was at peace again; her remarkable body had dispelled the fear in a way none of her friends could ever quite comprehend. Nicci was about to speak, but Keiko put a finger to her friend's lips.

"It is what friends do," Keiko whispered softly. "Now, Nicci, you must take us where we need to go." Moments later, the two of them were surveying the body of Lisa Tyrone, and, for the first time in her life, Keiko Tan wasn't sure she wanted to heal someone.

icci marveled at Keiko's seeming lack of fear when it came to using her empathic gifts. She never seemed to hesitate, never thought of herself or the pain that she was going to voluntarily assume on behalf of someone else. Nicci had wished, on more than one occasion, that she had Keiko's courage. She watched as the Asian girl studied Lisa Tyrone for a moment and then closed her eyes. Nicci assumed her friend was simply concentrating—preparing herself for the intensity of what was to come, but Nicci was wrong.

How would her friends feel, Keiko wondered, if they knew that there was a war going on inside of her right now? They would be shocked, she knew, to discover that she was hesitant to heal anyone, let alone Lisa. But she was, in fact, hesitating. The injuries to Lisa's body were so severe that Keiko was not certain she could heal the woman. She had never tried to aid anyone in such a dire situation; would she know if her own life was being endangered by the use of her empathic powers? Could she go too far in healing Lisa before realizing she did not have enough power left to save herself? Lisa Tyrone had once described Keiko's ability as a gift of pure selflessness best defined by the Greek word for the highest order of love: *agape*. Keiko's eyes misted at the memory of that conversation. She took a deep breath and began her work.

Keiko placed her hands an inch above Lisa's body and ran them across the woman's small frame—sensing the deepest and most life-threatening injuries. Swiftly and without hesitation now, Keiko placed her hands on either side of Lisa's face. She touched the flesh softly at first, and

Lisa's eyelashes fluttered for a moment as they had done earlier when Nicci had been near. Then, Keiko pressed a bit more firmly, and slowly the charred flesh of Lisa's face, which had broken open in some places and was oozing with a mixture of blood and other fluids, began to clear away. The layers of skin around her face began to regenerate as if they had simply been hidden by an ugly mask that was now coming off.

"Ohhhh!" Keiko fell to her knees, and Nicci knelt to steady her. It was unusual for Keiko to utter so much as the slightest cry of pain when she was using her ability. She held back any indication of her pain for fear the person she was aiding would feel guilty for causing another to suffer. Nicci felt certain that Lisa's injuries were far more serious than anything Keiko had attempted to deal with before. "Ooohhhh!" The girl cried again, a bit louder, and Nicci saw the lovely flesh of Keiko's face begin to mirror the burnt surface and open sores that had, only moments before, ravaged the face of Lisa Tyrone. Nicci took her friend's elbow gently, helped her to stand, and prepared to turn her away from the table for a few moments while her body healed itself; however, Keiko stepped out of the grasp and moved closer to Lisa Tyrone. "There is no time, Nicci. She is dying." And with that Keiko reached out to Lisa and placed her hands on the woman's chest—drawing out the fluid in her lungs and willing her heartbeat to become regular and steady.

The Asian girl began to shudder violently as Lisa's ailing health was drawn inside of her young body. "Keiko, stop it!" Nicci screamed, and her voice became one with the alarm which continued to beat throughout the corridors. "You can't do this much at once. You have to take time to recover first! Just for a few minutes. Please!"

And then, the alarm stopped. Nicci looked around but saw no movement. Keiko, though, sensed something. She looked up from her task, turned her back to the table, and slumped to the floor. Her arms were beginning to blacken, and the stench from her own burning flesh was filling the room. As her body began to heal itself, she became acutely aware of an emotion emanating from someone close by. It was *hate*. A deep, violent hatred. And now, *fear*, chill-you-to-the-bone kind of fear, coming from a completely different source. Click! A piece of metal seemed to unbolt and two more platforms, replicas of the one that held Lisa Tyrone, were rising from the floor. Dirk was shackled to one. On the other lay Mateo! Nicci gasped aloud in recognition and fright. Keiko shuddered involuntarily; she had found the source of the fear. Though both of the boys had been tightly gagged, their eyes effectively spoke of a terror few citizens of the Alliance had ever known—and none had lived to tell about. They were going to be *torched*.

Footsteps sounded in the corridor and within seconds there were Alliance guards blocking every exit. A tall, slender man stepped forward. He was clearly not one of the guards, for he was taller in stature and carried himself with a great deal of importance. There was very little in his physical appearance that distinguished him from the guards or Lisa Tyrone or any other member of the culture for that matter. His eyes were a deep blue, once a trait associated primarily with Caucasians but now shared by every human being. His sleek, jet-black hair had been engineered to reflect someone of Hispanic ancestry and looked no different from the hair of any person walking the streets of any town in any country of the world outside these walls. His skin would be most accurately described as mulatto, yet there was a deep chocolate tone to it, reminiscent of the African culture; it mirrored the skin color of every other member of society. And the almond shape of his eyes, as with the guards and Dr. Tyrone, paid tribute to those who were once defined as being of Asian descent. The Merger had brought a frightening sense of similarity to society.

Still, as this man came closer to Nicci, she noted that the alignment of his jaws seemed to come to a point at his chin. That, and the cold gaze he had fixed upon her, *did* distinguish him from others in the room. The guards, whose eyes were covered by face shields, remained alert but impassive. One could never know what they were thinking, unlike this man, whose primary thought and emotion had been sensed by Keiko only moments before. It was hate.

"My name, is Senator Broogue," he said icily. He regarded Nicci with a look of contempt and although his eyes remained fastened upon her, he addressed his next remark to Keiko. "Miss Tan, you will *cease* further use of your abilities for Dr. Tyrone's benefit at once." Keiko quickly masked her shock that this man *knew* of her abilities! How could he? No one, with the exception of Lisa Tyrone, would have any possible way to know of the teens' powers. She returned her attention to Lisa and avoided the Senator's prying eyes. "Ohhh, yes. I know about you, Miss Tan. I know more about you and your friends than even *you* know! Now, stop playing nurse, or you shall find out what happens *when I don't get what I want!*"

Nicci decided to try to draw his attention away from her friend. Perhaps Lisa could be stabilized if Keiko had a little more time. "So, are you the ringleader of this little circus event?" Nicci usually saved this challenging tone of voice for arguments with Matty and Dirk, but she did not think it wise to appear weak in front of this man. "I'd think you could find some better entertainment someplace else. You know that's Dr. Lisa Tyrone you've got strapped to that grill of yours, and she's a very influential person in the government, so you'd just better . . ."

The Senator cut into her banter with precision. "Dr. Tyrone is *no longer* an influential person, my dear. As I believe we are all well aware, she has been sought by the Alliance for crimes of the most serious nature for several years. Certainly you and your little band of *deviants* are aware of that. Now, before you decide to frighten me with your puny abilities, let me make something terribly clear—to *both* of you! No citizen of the Legion for World Alliance escapes the grasp of *justice.*" He raised his voice so that Keiko, who was continuing to ignore him, would hear. He looked to one of the guards and spoke with intensity, "Prepare them!"

At the Senator's word, the guard initiated a control, and the platforms containing Dirk and Mateo began moving along the floor and then, amazingly, up the wall! They stopped halfway up so that the boys were now facing out at the people in the room like some eerie type of three-dimensional wall-hangings. A moment later, a variety of mechanical arms came from the underside of the platforms and positioned the boys' legs so that they bent at the knee, forcing the soles of their bare feet flat against the tables. Another set of arms turned their heads, thrusting one side of their faces against the metal platforms so that their skin was pressed tightly against the cold steel surface. Next, their hands, palms down, were pressed flat against the table surface and held there. Several clicking sounds seemed to indicate that Dirk and Mateo were now locked into this position.

Keiko stepped away from Lisa. She sensed that to further challenge the Senator would bring harm to Dirk and Mateo, and she thought that she had done enough to stabilize the woman for a short time. Keiko faced the Senator, and he grimaced. "My dear girl, you look a fright!" he said maliciously. "I simply can't abide such ugliness. Go on about the business of doing something with yourself, won't you?" She stared him down. "Of course you will. Because *I* gave you a directive. And don't expect to hear anything from psycho-boy in your mind, if that's what you're waiting on. I've squelched all of that nonsense for several hours. My men in the lab have worked up a *nasty* little vial of liquid, and we've given a hefty dose to the boys. It will take care of their *abilities* for a good bit. Pity, I couldn't use it earlier because I needed to capture your little chameleon friend Mateo, and we had to let you retain your abilities until I had him."

Nicci saw the picture first. "You mean you *staged* all of this? You *let* me escape from my cell? You *knew* Dirk broke through the shield? You . . ."

"My dear, foolish girl. This is a *play,* and you've all performed exactly as I had hoped."

"But the alarm," Keiko stammered, the healing of her body now complete.

"Aaaaaahh! Yes, the alarm. Ingenious wasn't it? We set it off and left it on so that you would assume we were still after the shape-shifter. As long as you thought he was still free, you would likely remain here where we could keep an eye on you. If we had turned the alarm off, you might have realized we had him and tried to come to his aid. Actually, we caught him quite easily. A simple matter for a devious mind. I simply had the entire series of hallways surrounding your cell flooded with gas."

"But all of your men . . . they would have . . ." Keiko was getting a picture of just how ruthless Senator Broogue could be.

"Aaahh, sacrifices of war and all that. None of them died directly from exposure to the gas. A few concussions, a few broken bones from the falls when they passed out. Well, there was Gifford—hit the floor wrong when he fell—snapped his neck. But, I'm over my grief."

Nicci snapped. "How can you talk about people's lives as though they . . ."

"Miss Golden, I *hate* you!" There was nothing but scorn and loathing dripping from his voice. Then, quite suddenly, he spoke rather matter-of-factly. "Actually," he looked at Keiko, "I hate you both. I suppose if I'm entirely truthful, and perhaps that's best, I hate *all* of you."

"But why?" Keiko was genuinely saddened by the man's obvious malevolent nature.

"Because you are a threat to the Merger," he sneered.

Both Keiko and Nicci recognized the term from brief discussions during which the entire group had been successful in coaxing some information out of Lisa. They knew that the term *Merger* was used to describe an event—something that happened long ago which explained why the people looked the way they did—all the same—with the exception of gender. They also felt certain, though Lisa had never confirmed it, that had the Merger not occurred, there would be others whose appearance was unique. Others like the four of them.

"The Alliance has worked too hard to forge this world anew. And you, the four of you and Dr. Tyrone, are a threat to it." The Senator paced like a general providing details to his troops. "The problem, as I see it, is that you'd rather protect your own precious lives than sacrifice them for the good of an entire world. Don't you see the damage you've done? Look at these men!" He pointed to the guards all around the room. "I'm going to kill them all just as soon as I finish with you. I *have* to because they know about you. They're not supposed to know that you exist, but they do, and therefore they are all going to die. None of them are going home to their families tonight, Miss Tan, Miss Golden, simply because *you* exist."

The guards clearly heard what the Senator said, but there was no conscious acknowledgment of it that Keiko or Nicci could see.

"Now then," Senator Broogue began again. "We are ever at work—improving the Torcher, as you may have heard. I've been especially anxious to try out this latest modification. I do believe it's going to be delicious fun!" He addressed the guard again, "Sir, if you will do the honors." As Nicci and Keiko watched, a yellowish liquid began to pour out onto the platforms to which their friends were shackled; however, it did not run off or down the sides toward the floor as one would expect. Rather it seemed drawn, almost through some kind of magnetic pull, to the sides of the boys' faces that were touching the platform surface and to the palms of their hands and the soles of their feet. It seeped underneath those specific areas of their skin and eventually could be seen no more.

The girls regarded Senator Broogue, who was only too happy to provide an explanation. He grinned with devilish delight. "It's a special kind of *oil,*" he said. "We've been working on it for quite some time, and it's just now ready for testing. I do believe it's going to be a most effective means of punishment. And best of all, it will hasten the torching process. Rather than simply heating flesh through our infrared technology, we'll be heating the oil first . . . and that will result in a much more painful experience. Let's give it a whirl, shall we?" He spoke as if they might all board a carnival ride at any moment.

"You *can't* be serious!" Keiko cried. "You don't *really* want to do this!"

The Senator ignored her and walked up a short set of stairs to Dirk and Mateo. The profiles of the boys' faces communicated their fury as he cast a cool glance of appraisal at each of them. "Mr. Tyrone." Malice dripped from the Senator's lips like an ice cream cone in a summer heat wave. "I *wonder* if you've ever seen meat frying on a grill! Ever thought about what that might feel like, Mr. Rodriguez? The heat? That popping, sizzling sound? The sight of *flames* occasionally bursting forth?" The boys' eyes were wide with terror, but the slightest attempt at a struggle was useless. They were locked into position with no hope of escape.

Keiko could feel hatred swelling within their adversary. Whatever action he intended to take, it would happen soon. "Please, Senator Broogue. You're such a powerful man, surely . . ."

"Don't play psychological games with me, Miss Tan!" He thrust a finger at her accusingly, and she stepped back. "Now, boys," the Senator sneered with amusement as he turned his back on Mateo and Dirk, "you're going to experience a barbecue from a whole new perspective!" He spun around and glared at one of the guards. "DO IT!" He howled vindictively, and seconds later half of Dirk's face could be heard sizzling on the platform. The boy cried out through the gag in horror as his hands and feet followed suit. "Now, quickly, the other one, too!" cried the Senator. Mateo's body trembled in agony as he, too, felt his flesh cooking. Their tormentor's eyes were dancing with delight as he looked for a brief moment at the girls. "If either of you moves a muscle," he warned, "I'll fry their entire bodies all at once."

Abruptly, a tiny shimmering particle of light sped into the room like a comet gone wild. It grew, exponentially, until an aura burst forth creating a transparent circle of gold; within it stood three figures. The tallest, a woman, stood in the center of the three and wore a robe of white silk. Her skin color was a perfect match to Nicci's. To her right stood a man wearing a white lab coat and trousers. He had a stethoscope around his neck and was fidgeting with it nervously. He was fully Asian—like Keiko. The third figure was changing shape so quickly it was impossible to tell anything for sure other than that she was female. As the aura evaporated, she lost her human form entirely, transforming into a lion nearly twice the size of the typical jungle cat. A thunderous roar filled the room as the animal leapt with incredible speed and agility upon Senator Broogue, knocking him forcefully to the ground. "Turn off the grills, Senator. This cook-out is over!" The great cat eyed the Senator as it spoke. Then, it snarled, bared its teeth, and moved threateningly close to the man's neck.

CHAPTER 4

The guards stood motionless as Senator Broogue called to them, "Shoot! Kill!" Nothing. "The guards are useless, Senator," the white-robed woman spoke with great authority. "They are frozen in time and will not move again until I deem it necessary. Now, I suggest you do as my companion suggested. I will release Mr. Larson," she indicated one of the guards, "as I believe he is the one you need to stop that horrific device; however, he will move only as long as I allow it." The lion lifted its head and roared with tremendous force—lending support to the woman's command—and when its paw came down, one of the claws inched its way into the Senator's chest.

"Stop the Torcher, Mr. Larson, for the moment." The Senator's voice showed no sign of fear, but rather a healthy respect for the power of these beings. Larson did as he was instructed but did not move again.

Nicci marveled that this woman, towering above everyone in her white robe and with skin as dark as Nicci's, also possessed the ability to manipulate time. It couldn't be a coincidence—the similarity. Their roles within their respective groups were different, though, Nicci reminded herself. This woman was the *leader* of her group. Whether official or unofficial, Nicci could not be sure, but there was no denying that the other two were taking their cues from her. Within her own group of friends, Dirk would be the one they would look to for leadership. It had never been put to the test because Lisa had always been there—acting as their parental figure; nevertheless, Nicci knew it was true: Dirk would lead if a leader were called for, and all of them would follow him. She was distracted, for a moment, by the thought of what he had done to her earlier—forcing her to move through time and find his aunt—without even pausing for a discussion. It was a side of Dirk she had never imagined. Before this, she would have followed him without question . . . but now? Now, she was no longer certain.

Nicci was brought back to the moment as the regal woman adjusted her robe, gracefully inclined her head toward the only male member of her group, and spoke. "*Dr. Pan,* if you would be so kind." She was inviting her associate to do something, but Nicci had no idea what it might be. Keiko, on the other hand, had an idea. She could sense the power within him—power that exceeded her own healing abilities in both depth and breadth.

"Why, yes, Margaret . . . er . . . I mean *Madam Moment,* of course, of course!" His enthusiasm for the task, whatever it was to be, was apparent as his face broke into a wide grin. Keiko noted that Dr. Pan had stopped fiddling with the stethoscope that had so preoccupied him ever since he and his friends had appeared. As she surveyed him carefully, she stifled a giggle. He was a short and stocky fellow who wore a strap around his head with a small round mirror attached to the front. On the outer pocket of his white coat the title *Dr. Panacea* was embroidered in blue letters, and she noted that the pocket appeared to be filled with tongue depressors. She nearly wondered aloud if he had lollipops for everyone who behaved well!

His skin and hair color, as well as the shape of his eyes, were identical to Keiko's. This was the first time any of them had seen another person with whom they shared the physical characteristics that set them apart from every member of their own society. Keiko found a special comfort in the quality of sameness she shared with the doctor and sensed great joy in him as he prepared to use his abilities. She watched with amazement as he stretched his hands forward, directing one toward Dirk, the other toward Mateo, and closed his eyes. Surely he would need physical contact with them in order to heal them—just as she did. She had never considered attempting to heal from a distance. Could it be possible? It appeared so—for in mere seconds he seemed to finish his task, and the soft groans and movements from Dirk and Mateo indicated the work of the Torcher had been reversed. Amazingly, Dr. Pan had absorbed the boys' injuries in seconds, yet he displayed no outward signs of having done so. Keiko marveled at his power.

Dr. Pan turned to the woman he had addressed as Madam Moment and chuckled with delight. "There you are, Madam! Good as new! Good as new!" Suddenly, he began fumbling with his stethoscope as if troubled and spoke to her conspiratorially, "I can't get them loose from that contraption, you know."

Madam Moment smiled at him tolerantly. "Yes, Doctor, I was getting to that. *Mrs. Morph,*" she addressed the great jungle cat, "your assistance with the boys, please. I'll take care of Senator Broogue," she said and focused a hand toward him that seemed to hold him at bay.

Instantaneously, the lion transformed into a gorilla that began growing larger and larger until the growth spurt seemed, literally, out of control. Its head and shoulders crashed unceremoniously through the roof of the security complex, producing screams of panic from people on the street. Madam Moment appeared unnerved. "Oh, Mrs. Morph, *really!* Must you always overdo? One of these days your flamboyant nature is going to get you into some trouble that I can't get you out of! To business if you will. I can't hold this all together for an unlimited amount of time, though *time* is my specialty."

She addressed Nicci and Keiko for the first time. The two girls, though not frozen like the guards, had found that they did not want to move and wouldn't have known where to go if they had. These strangers clearly had abilities similar to their own, but they were obviously much more powerful. The real question was, were they friends? "Come ladies," Madam Moment beckoned. "Down here if you would. We must leave quickly." The woman cast a nervous glance toward the Senator that did not go unnoticed by Keiko.

The giant shrunk to a more manageable size and ripped the metal bonds from Dirk and Mateo as if they were made of plastic. Mateo yanked the gag from his mouth, "Let's get outta here and fast!" He and Dirk stepped down to join the others just as Mrs. Morph returned to human form. She was much more colorful than her colleagues, clothed in a garish green jumpsuit with a pattern of stripes not unlike that of a zebra running through the cloth. As Dirk drew close, Keiko noticed no scarring of any kind on his body. She smiled thankfully at Dr. Panacea, who grinned and gave her a small wave. Dirk looked toward his aunt, still shackled to one of the Torchers, and all eyes followed his lead.

Madam Moment questioned the doctor. "Can she be saved?" Somehow, by the tone in her voice, they all knew what the response would be. Dr. Panacea's lower lip burst forth a bit. He reached nervously for his stethoscope and looked at the ground. "No, Madam. It is too late. I can't save her." He looked at Dirk and his friends, and spoke apologetically, "Sometimes, healing comes from letting go. What I can do now would only sustain her suffering."

"She can't *die!* Is that what you're telling us—that she's going to die? Because she can't!" Mateo, impulsive as ever, raced to where Lisa's still form lay on the platform. "Surely, you people can do something. We've seen what you can do! You *can* do it. You just *won't!* You probably . . ."

"Matty," Keiko had not moved from where she stood. "Don't lash out. They have shown kindness and generosity. They saved both you and Dirk. Surely they would save Lisa if they could do so."

Nicci looked to Madam Moment and inclined her head toward Dirk who had become a silent statue. "She's his aunt, you know. Doesn't he even get to say goodbye? She's the only mother any of us has ever known! What are we supposed to do . . . just *leave her here?*" Nicci's voice came across a bit more challenging than she had intended, but a part of her wondered if Matty was right—maybe these people *were* allowing Lisa to die.

Dr. Pan looked to Madam Moment. "Their hearts are so heavy. Couldn't we just . . ."

"A moment," Madam declared. "They shall have a *moment* in time. It will run its course rapidly, though, for *time* is a fleeting thing."

Dirk noted that Madam Moment did not direct her attention from Senator Broogue for more than a few seconds as she spoke. While the Alliance guards were frozen in time, her hold on the Senator was different. Though he could not move physically, he seemed to be challenging her in some way. Yes. Something unspoken was going on between these two powerful figures—something much more than what was apparent on the surface. Madam Moment and Senator Broogue were not meeting for the first time. Dirk was certain of that. He was also keenly aware that his friends all had a counterpart in this amazing group of newcomers—someone who shared their physical appearances and their powers. He was the only exception, and it bothered him. He wondered why, yet he was unsure if he really wanted to know the answer.

Madam's firm voice broke into his thoughts as she addressed him and his friends. "Remember this. *Time* is a precious commodity. Do not waste it! You are about to move neither into the past nor toward the future, but instead to a moment in time that has been crafted just for you. Use it well." Keeping one hand trained on the Senator, she brought forth the other and with a flick of her wrist altered the whereabouts of Lisa Tyrone, her nephew, and his companions.

Dirk immediately recognized the surroundings—this picnic spot held many memories for all of them. It was the one
outdoor location that Lisa had deemed safe enough for them
to spend time together. It had been home to many games of
tag and story readings and the site of countless requests by
Matty for Lisa to let them have a dog. A tattered green blan-
ket lay against a grassy surface that didn't quite match it in
color. A brisk breeze brought warm air across the valley and
into the pine forest that had always provided both protection and concealment for the group. His aunt was passing
paper plates to all of them—and she looked fine. It seemed
so real! Dirk looked across to Keiko and saw a puzzled
expression on her face. He then touched the minds of both
Mateo and Nicci and realized that they were thinking, as he
was, that although the surroundings were familiar, they
were *not* reliving a memory from the past.

Lisa Tyrone took a container out of the basket, opened her
mouth to speak, and paused. She pursed her lips for a
moment and set the container back into the basket. Then,
she raised her eyes and looked at the four young people seated in a circle around her. Though none of them were born to
her, they were *all* her children. As she had told them many
times, "Giving birth isn't what makes you a mother; it's
everything that comes after."

"Kids, we have to have a serious talk, and *time* is short.
I'm dying . . . you all know that. We aren't really at the picnic spot. Well, I suppose we *are here* in a sense, but we're
also inside one of the Alliance's security complexes." As soon
as she spoke the words, reality set in and the memory of the
day's events was triggered with painful accuracy in Dirk
and his friends.

Mateo was the first to speak. "Lisa, you're okay! We can
see you. Your body is fine. They fixed you up!"

"Aunt Lisa," Dirk grabbed her hand protectively. "You look
fine. Matty's right. They healed *us*. They must have . . ." His

voice trailed off as tears welled in Keiko's eyes. Lisa looked away from her nephew for a moment but squeezed his hand tightly.

"Dirk," Keiko tried to control her voice, to keep it from trembling. "*I* could not save her. *They* could not save her. These beings, whoever they are, have given her the appearance of health, but it is a fantasy."

Lisa Tyrone reached up and ran a hand tenderly down the side of her nephew's face. "Keiko's right, Dirk. We are here," she was gazing at all of them as she spoke, "to say goodbye."

CHAPTER 5

"She's right." Nicci jumped in before Dirk or Mateo could speak. "Let's not waste our time arguing about it."

Lisa turned back to them. Her face was all business; she did not, however, release Dirk's hand. As Nicci was in reach, she grasped her hand as well. "Listen to me very carefully, kids. I've spent my life protecting you and loving you because you are very special young people. I wouldn't trade my decisions for anything. But now you have to move on without me, and you can. You *must*." Her voice took on an urgency of purpose that kept the rapt attention of each of the teens. "The beings who appeared in the complex are incredibly powerful, but they aren't powerful enough, on their own, to reverse the effects of the Merger."

"Reverse the Merger? Lisa, are you *crazy?* How could anyone . . ."

"Matty, listen to me," she continued. "This is going to be very hard for you to understand, but I give you my word that it *is* the truth. The Merger exists because time has been altered."

"Whoa, slow down, Lisa. I know a little bit about time," Nicci began, "but what do you mean by *altered?*"

"Nicci . . . kids," Lisa leaned forward. "Our world was never *meant* to be like this. The merging of races into a society filled with people who look like me should *never* have occurred. In the timeline we were meant to live in, the Merger would never have existed."

"You mean . . ." Mateo started to interrupt, but she cut him off.

"What I'm telling you is that someone traveled back into

history, far back into the past of our world, and altered the timeline. Whatever was altered set the stage for a *merging* of races. You must understand that the world you were born into is the result of someone tampering with the past!"

Dirk's mind was spinning. One part of him was lost in a sea of grief that threatened with each passing second to grab him and pull him under. How could anything happen to his Aunt Lisa? She was supposed to live forever. Another part of him was deeply involved in her story and wanted to ask a thousand questions. Only one came out. "How do you know this?"

"Sweetheart," she said, releasing his hand, "I've known since the day you were all born. The beings you encountered today appeared before me at the hospital within a few hours of your births. They referred to themselves as the *Elders* and told me a story of the past in much more detail than I have time to tell you now. But the important thing, the *most important thing* is that you four survive. It was critical then, and that's why they came to me. Their directions to me were very specific, and I just had this *sense* that what they were telling me was the truth. I can't explain it. They named each of you—names that reflected your hidden family lineages.

"Are you sayin' the lady in the zebra outfit named me instead of you?" Mateo blustered.

"Matty!" Nicci's frustration with her friend was showing. "Would you focus on the *important* issues? Lisa, what do you mean by *hidden* family lineages?"

"She's saying," Keiko interjected, "that my parents *were* Asian. But they never knew it?"

"No one knows. Well, almost no one," Lisa said boldly. "The entire society has been genetically engineered to look the way that they do, and it's been that way for so long." She paused as if lost in thought. "The people have no idea of their true racial characteristics. No one knows the details of how or even when this all began except the Senator and a few of his associates. A handful of doctors and scientists like me are told as much as I'm sharing with you now, but they only tell us because they need our skills if and when something unexpected happens."

"Something unexpected like *us*—you mean?" Dirk spat the words out. He felt a surge of anger that his aunt had withheld so much from them for all these years. "I don't get *how* people can't know their race is being hidden. And *where* is it being hidden? Is it actually *underneath* what we see? *When* is it done to them? *How* is it done? *Why* didn't it work on us?"

"Dirk," she said sorrowfully, "the Alliance has developed a scientific process that alters DNA, and they've come as close as they can to perfecting it while babies are still in the womb."

Nicci couldn't believe what she was hearing. "So mothers just allow some freaky scientists and doctors to . . ."

"There isn't time to give you all of the details of how it's accomplished, Nicci," Lisa explained. The reality is that they've succeeded in creating a world with no racial diversity and no racial *adversity*. Whether that's a good thing or a bad thing is an issue you can form your own opinions about, but it's a fact; moreover, it's a *secret*—kept from the people—a secret the Alliance is more than willing to kill to keep."

"But there is hope," Lisa continued. "The Elders. *They* are the reason I took you into hiding; they're the reason I've spent my life protecting you from the Alliance. I knew they would return someday when the time was right. That day is today. Your survival is even more critical now because you're finally old enough to do what needs to be done, and they will help you."

"But Lisa, why are *we* so critical? I mean we have these abilities, but what can we, how can we . . ." Keiko struggled to form a coherent question.

"Keiko, there is a task ahead for all of you. It will be

explained more fully later by the Elders, but believe me when I tell you that you are the only hope for our world. If you don't succeed in this endeavor, our people will continue to live with no knowledge of history, no sense of identity, and no hope for the future."

Suddenly time shifted and for a brief second the picnic scene began to fade. At that moment, Lisa's skin began to blacken. Dirk steadied her as she began to fall. "Ohhhh!" She gasped, and her face grew taut with pain.

Mateo jumped to his feet, "What's happening, man? Nicci, are you . . ." But before he could finish his sentence, their surroundings grew stable once more, and Lisa seemed to strengthen.

She gestured for Mateo to sit. "Matty, you're going to have to curb that impulsive nature one of these days. You promise?"

"I'll work on it, Lisa. I'm *always* working on it." He gave her the Cheshire grin that she loved. She had told him from the time he was little of the story of Alice in Wonderland, and how he, like the Cheshire cat, had an unforgettable smile.

As Mateo sat, Lisa began to speak quickly. "The Elders will take care of you. Kids—go with them. *Trust them* as you would me."

"Trust is *built,* Lisa," Keiko said wisely. "You taught us that."

"Yes, Keiko, I did. If you can't trust them, then trust me. Everything within me from the moment they first appeared tells me that they are here to help you—to help our world. But there is another, a fourth being. He is incredibly powerful and very dangerous. They said very little about him—only that he is the one responsible for altering time. He knows about you, the four of you. You are a *threat* to him. I believe he . . . aaaaahhh!" Dr. Tyrone raised her hands to the sides of her head and shook it from side to side—not so much in pain as in annoyance at first. Then, the pain came, and she cried out.

"Aunt Lisa?" Dirk questioned.

"My mind . . . I . . . it feels like someone is . . ."

Dirk thrust himself to his aunt's mental aid and was immediately struck down by a forceful blow. It felt as if a wall of bricks had collapsed on top of him. Instinctively, he recoiled to the privacy of his own mind.

Lisa seemed to get a moment's reprieve and her final words came tumbling forth, "I will be with you always . . . always. Remember that you are each other's . . ."

Before the phrase could be completed an indescribable torrent of wind seemed to whisk them away from the picnic setting and into a state of chaos. It felt as though they were falling through time and space. Screams of panic from Nicci ignited the air as she fought unsuccessfully to stabilize their movement. Darkness surrounded them and a deep and evil laughter, dripping with rancor, burst into their conscious minds and sent chills up and down their spines.

"Come here, boy." The laughter ceased from inside Dirk's mind and was replaced by a frighteningly powerful voice. Dirk tried to force it away, but it was far too powerful. He sensed it somehow separating him from the others, and then, abruptly, he stopped falling. Now, he was hanging, and it felt like something enormous was holding him up by the back of his shirt. His feet dangled helplessly over nothingness. The blackness still surrounded him but a small amount of light began to slowly illuminate a living creature that was holding him. It was a huge giant with enormous gaping eyes and a ferocious set of teeth. Fairy tales, particularly *Jack and the Beanstalk,* had always fascinated Dirk. As he was growing up, he had frequently fancied himself as Jack—climbing the beanstalk and running from the evil giant, but there had always been an element of fear there. What if there really *were* giants? It had never been monsters or clowns that sought Dirk in his nightmares; it had *always* been giants.

And the giant who held him now, in what was a very awkward position for Dirk, was acting a lot like the giants of Dirk's boyhood nightmares. "My, my, my," said a voice that Dirk recognized as the source of the evil laughter he had heard just moments before. "You're looking terribly *tasty* tonight." The giant made a slurping noise and eyed Dirk craftily. The timbre of the voice seemed to have changed. Now, it sounded, oddly enough, like the voice of Senator Broogue! "I think it's time for *dinner,*" the giant said and licked his lips, emphasizing that Dirk was about to become the main course.

A part of Dirk knew that there was really no giant. This was all in his mind—something or some*one* was exerting incredible power to create all of this. And though he believed it wasn't real, Dirk felt certain that he was, in fact, in terrible danger. Landing in the giant's mouth, he knew, would somehow end his life. The giant roared, raised Dirk higher, tilted his enormous head back, and opened his wide, cavernous mouth. Streams of saliva were dripping from the inside and collecting on his tongue in anticipation of Dirk's arrival, and the points of the razor-sharp teeth glistened.

This was *exactly* the way it always had happened for Dirk. It was as if one of his childhood nightmares had been taken from his mind and brought to life in a very realistic forum. Then, he was falling again, only this time there was a clear, if unattractive, destination. He fought in vain to somehow reach into and control the giant's mind, but just as he realized the futility of his struggle, a presence arrived that swept him away to safety. The giant roared in fury and grabbed greedily for Dirk, but the boy knew he would not be recaptured. Madam Moment had come to his rescue.

The two of them materialized in an underground chamber

shortly after the others. As he looked around, Dirk noticed a
table and chairs, but the walls and floors appeared to be
those of a cave. He eyed the chairs a second time—there
were only enough for the people who were present. Pangs of
grief swelled within him; there was no seat for his aunt. The
finality of her absence was now unavoidable. His eyes flickered toward Mateo.

"Dirk, man, are you okay? We were worried. I mean they
showed up and all," he gestured to Dr. Pan and Mrs. Morph,
"and we were with them, but no one knew where *you* were.
You were with us in the picnic area, but then . . ."

Dirk put a hand on Mateo's shoulder. "I'm fine, Matty. I
had a little unexpected dinner date is all." He looked warily
across the cave toward the Elders. "Anyone want to tell me
what that was all about?"

"What? Did I miss something? I missed something, didn't
I? What happened to the kiddo? Ya gotta tell me when I miss
something!" Mrs. Morph cracked a piece of gum noisily and
glanced sideways at Dr. Pan while sauntering over to
inspect Dirk. The boy took a step back. He was not at all certain what to make of this woman. While the good-natured
Dr. Pan and the regal Madam Moment seemed entirely
trustworthy, the woman her colleagues called Mrs. Morph
was quite another matter. First, she didn't *talk* like the others; she spoke with no sense of formality. In fact, her speech
sounded more like that of a street-smart, wisecracking ado-
lescent. Her clothes (she was no longer wearing the zebra
outfit) were another matter that led Dirk to question her
authenticity as a friend. She was dressed, now, in a "leopard"
jumpsuit. She wore a purple beret on her head with a thin
black-and-white-striped veil attached to it. Large horn-
rimmed glasses drew attention to her eyes, and the purse
she was carrying matched her orange and turquoise shoes
perfectly.

She looked much younger than her companions, and her

olive skin, dark hair, and brown eyes were a match with
Mateo's. "Come on, kiddos. You can trust me. All right, so I
may not be the girl you'd bring home to mother and all, but I
know how to have a good time. If ya know what I mean."
Pause. She looked toward Madam Moment and issued a frus-
trated plea. "Tell 'em I'm okay, Margie; they're really worried."

"Mrs. *Morph!*" Madam raised her voice. "Need I remind
you of our agreement *not* to use first names? Besides, I have
repeatedly assured you that my name is *Margaret,* and if
you can't remember to call me . . ."

"Okay, okay, okay. Ya don't gotta go on the lecture circuit
over it. I'm tellin' ya, there's too much goin' on up here in the
old noggin for me to keep track of all these details. I ain't
never been a detail-type girl—if ya know what I mean." Mrs.
Morph appeared oblivious to the fact that she had both
interrupted her friend and delivered this entire response to
the interior of her purse where she was rummaging about
with great commotion. At last, she pulled out a package of
chewing gum. *"Juicy Juicy!* I need a booster shot. Ya want
some?" She offered a piece to Dirk, who continued to keep
his distance from her. She sighed with exasperation. "Cut
me a little slack will ya, kiddo? Margie—ya gotta tell the
kiddos that I'm on the level."

Madam Moment pulled out a chair and gestured for all to
be seated. "Mrs. Morph is a bit eccentric. She is also much
older than she appears, but given her unique abilities, her
physical appearance is within her control." One look at Mrs.
Morph's face told them that this was information she didn't
want publicized. "Appearances are terribly important to her
as you can see by her . . . *attire.*" Madam Moment's voice
betrayed a bit of sarcasm as she referred to her companion's
wardrobe, and Nicci stifled a giggle. "But she is, in every
sense of the word, a loyal member of our group."

"Okay then," said Dirk impetuously. "What happened to
us back there? What happened to *me* back there?"

"Mr. Tyrone!" Madam Moment's voice was clipped. "Your tone will be excused because you are understandably distraught over the death of your aunt." All eyes looked down with the exception of Dirk. He kept his gaze level with Madam. "She *is* gone, yes."

Keiko began to weep softly, and Dr. Pan reached for her hand. "You know, child," he said gently, "that there was nothing more to be done. That is sometimes the way of things."

Nicci, for the first time, considered traveling into the past. She had never done so, yet escaping this cave right now, fleeing from the news of Lisa's death, seemed so right. If she could travel to a time in the past, when Lisa was alive and healthy, she could hide from the truth. She raised her eyes to find Madam staring her full in the face and shaking her head. Permission denied.

Mateo jumped up from his seat, and in his pupils they all saw the image of a polar bear. A second later, the boy was gone—and the bear, standing on its hind legs, had replaced him. It began pacing. "Oh, this is *great!* This is *just* great. You just deliver the news that . . . well, you deliver this kind of news, and we're supposed to what—just believe you?" The bear slapped one paw on its head and then raised it off in a gesture filled with sarcasm. "Oh, I forgot, we're supposed to just trust you because you *kidnapped* us and brought us to a cave with a table and some chairs that aren't even that comfortable!"

"Matty," Keiko spoke with more force than usual—even as tears continued to roll down her cheeks. "We should trust them because Lisa asked us to."

Mateo looked to Dirk. "Well, what do you say? Do *you* trust them?"

Dirk's anger and uncertainty exploded at his friend. "How should *I* know who to trust . . . or what to believe! And what would it matter if I did, Matty? You think I can just step into the shoes of my *dead aunt* and make all the decisions now?

Is *that* what you all think?" Dirk pointed to his chest with intensity. "Well if that's what you think, then you're wrong. I'm not your leader. Never have been, and I'm sure not gonna start now."

The bear issued a frightening roar in response and looked savagely at Dirk. "I was askin' for your *opinion!* That's it. Nobody needs you to *lead* them anywhere, mister high-and-mighty! I want action, and I want answers. Now!"

Madam Moment's face revealed her lack of patience. "Sit," she commanded Mateo. He roared in response, and Mrs. Morph quickly removed a nail file from her purse and began filing furiously. "I said *sit* down, Mr. Rodriguez." Madam's tone was undeniably firm. Nicci felt as if they should all stand and then sit again just to demonstrate respect for the woman's authority.

When Mateo did not move, Mrs. Morph looked up quickly from her filing. "Listen, kid, gettin' Margie all fired up is *not* gonna win ya any popularity votes, and it's gonna end up gettin' yours truly in a heap a trouble. If ya sit down, I'll teach ya how to speed up your transformations—geez you're slow! And *what's* with that eye thing? Ya want the whole world to know what you're gonna become? I can see I got my work cut out for me."

The bear transformed back into Mateo, who sat next to Mrs. Morph and challenged, "What do you mean I'm *slow!* I'm not slow. I'm . . ."

"What you *are,* Mr. Rodriguez," said Madam, "is not in a position of authority here. The information you feel you are due will be explained to you but *not* because you have demanded it. Answers will be provided because without them, the four of you will be unable to complete your task."

"And just what might that be, if you don't mind my asking?" Nicci's voice held curiosity but no malice. She looked steadily into the older woman's eyes. Madam Moment was the first person Nicci had ever seen who shared her physical attributes, and there was something comforting about that. She assumed Keiko and Mateo felt the same about the other Elders—their counterparts.

The older woman regarded Nicci thoughtfully. "Your task, Miss Golden, is to undo what has been done. To remove what has been manufactured and to put back in place what is natural. You will restore the unique facet of *race* to this world again, and in doing so, you will *destroy* the Merger."

CHAPTER 6

The rapt attention of the entire group, with the exception of Mrs. Morph, who was once again busying herself in her purse, was directed at Madam Moment. "You are wondering, no doubt, why your final moments with Lisa Tyrone were so violently shattered? The answer is simple and not simple. The simple answer is that the being . . ." She paused as if she were about to say something more but chose not to. "The *best* answer is that I lost control over Senator Broogue, and he attempted an attack on the four of you simultaneously. When that effort failed, he separated you, Mr. Tyrone, from the group and sought to use a creation of your own mind to destroy you."

Dirk leaned forward and rested his elbows on the table. "I *knew* it was in my mind, but it was so real! I can't understand how it could have all been my imagination." Then, a thought struck him. "Wait a minute—the Senator controlled *my* mind? How could anyone?" Finally, it dawned on him. "He's the fourth one, isn't he? The Senator's *my* counterpart! He looked at his friends. "You all have one, an Elder who's like you . . . but not me. And I wondered why. Now I know. I *do* have one; it's just that he's evil." Dirk's mind was flowing like a rushing current—so many thoughts, moving so rapidly, and he was allowing his stream of consciousness to be heard by all of them. "But he doesn't look like me. I mean his skin isn't like mine, and his eyes aren't . . ." He stopped as he saw the look of consternation on Madam's face.

Mrs. Morph did not look up from her purse but assessed the situation skillfully. "Ya gotta learn when to keep quiet, kiddo. Margie isn't the kinda girl who gets interrupted. Why I remember this one time when I was tryin' to . . ."

"That will do, Mrs. Morph," Madam said with exasperation.

Mrs. Morph looked at Dirk and his friends. *"That will do. If I had a dollar for every time I've heard that, I could do some serious . . ."*

"Mrs. Morph!"

"Yeah, okay, okay. I know. Respect your elders. Ya gotta admit though, Margie, I'm doin' better."

Madam did not respond to her colleague but kept her attention focused on Dirk and his friends. "What I'm telling you, telling *all* of you, is that the one who is seeking you out is extremely powerful and more dangerous than you can even begin to imagine. Mr. Tyrone, you did not *imagine* the giant who sought to devour you. The being you know as Senator Broogue took your greatest nightmare and physically became it. He was the giant of your dreams, but I assure you that your death, a very real death, was imminent if I had not arrived when I did."

Mateo's Cheshire grin appeared despite his best efforts to look serious. "So, you're sayin' that the boogeyman might try and pull me under my bed tonight and strangle me?"

Mrs. Morph winced and shook her head vigorously but did not look up. "Not a good move, kiddo, I wouldn'ta said that, not for a million—and I'm the kinda girl who speaks her mind."

Madam Moment's voice became edgy. "I can *assure* you, Mr. Rodriguez, that if the Senator takes an interest in this 'boogeyman' as you call him, you shall not be smiling for long. Nor shall you sleep soundly . . . or safely."

The pause in conversation allowed Keiko to gently address Madam Moment. "You said 'the being *we know* as Senator Broogue.' Madam, who is he really?"

At this, Mrs. Morph looked up instantly and fixed a gaze upon her colleague. Dr. Pan took some tongue depressors out of his coat pocket and began counting them, but he, too,

regarded Madam Moment with interest. When she did not
speak, he looked down at the table and very quietly said, "I
think you should tell them, Madam."

A weighted sigh was released from the white-robed Elder,
and finally she spoke again. "Senator Broogue, for lack of a
better title, is . . . *was* one of us."

The teens' eyes grew wide. Nicci gasped audibly but did
not interrupt.

"Yes. There were four of us just as there are four of you.
Surely you've noticed that we are, in a sense, counterparts.
Mr. Tyrone, you are correct. Senator Broogue is your coun-
terpart."

Dirk countered for argument's sake, "But he's *merged*. His
skin isn't white like mine. We saw him." He looked at his
friends for support. "You guys saw him, right?"

"Sure, the guy looks just like everybody else—present
company excluded," said Mateo.

"Dirk, allow Madam to finish her explanation," Keiko suggested.

Mrs. Morph eyed Keiko craftily. "You're gonna be her
favorite, kiddo. You understand how she likes doin' business."

Madam Moment tilted her head at her colleague.
"Favoritism! Mrs. Morph, really!"

Dr. Panacea became restless in his seat—drawing
everyone's attention toward him. He seemed most anxious
as he spoke of Senator Broogue. "He *appears* to be merged,
Dirk, but he is not. His racial profile is the same as yours;
he is Caucasian." Dr. Pan identified Dirk's race with little
more than a whisper, and his eyes darted around the room
nervously as if speaking of the Senator might actually cause
the man to appear before them.

Nicci was bursting with questions. "How is it that the
Senator appears merged, but none of you do?"

"Appears is the key word, Sweetie!" Mrs. Morph blew a

quick bubble and popped it. "He just shows you what he wants you to see—or hides what he doesn't want you to see." Mrs. Morph transformed into an exact replica of the Senator for a moment and then adjusted the form to show him as a Caucasian. Mateo noted that the Senator's image was not revealed in the pupils of her eyes before the transformation. Clearly, her skills were far advanced when compared with his own.

"In order for you to begin preparing for the task ahead, you will need a lesson in history," Madam announced. "You need to know of the world before the Merger. You need to know of our history and that of the Senator in order to understand what transpired to bring about the merged race that now exists. Doctor, if you would please, begin."

It seemed to Keiko that her counterpart was anticipating being called upon. As he rose, she had the sense that the three Elders were following a scripted plan, that they had known the time for this "talk" would come and each of them had a specific role to play.

Dr. Pan looked deeply saddened as he spoke. "Long ago the world was made up of many races; yet there was not always harmony. In some countries, cities, and villages, differences in race caused fear and distrust. Sometimes violence erupted, sometimes war."

"War?" Nicci was astounded. "Just because people didn't *look* the same? That's crazy! I guess one benefit of merging races was to stop the fighting."

Dr. Pan's face hardened. "There will *always* be differences between people, Nicci, and those differences will always make themselves known. Hiding physical differences does not make us more alike; it simply masks the truth. The Merger is the manifestation of people's hatred and fear of what is different in one another, and nothing good can come from that. A society cannot grow to appreciate something they cannot see."

Keiko tugged lightly at the doctor's lab coat. "But Doctor Pan, how did all of you become involved in this? Were you in a war?"

The doctor seated himself again and patted her hand. "I suppose, in a way, we were." He sighed heavily, but Madam nodded for him to continue. "All of our parents, including the Senator's, were scientists—leading scientists in their respective countries. The common thread in their work was the study of human DNA and the effects that exposure to different types of microorganisms might have on people. That shared interest brought them to the United States when we were all very young children. They worked as a team in a program funded internationally."

"Impressive," Mateo said sincerely.

"Ha! Sounds better than it was, kiddo," Mrs. Morph chimed in. "Ya shoulda seen our housing." She poked his arm with her index finger. "I never seen bugs that big anywhere else; I'm here ta tell ya that right now!"

Dr. Pan began to narrate again. "The research facility was in a fairly small town in the southwestern U.S. Conditions weren't ideal, always, that's true, but our parents became more than colleagues—they became friends."

"As did we," Madam picked up the story seamlessly. "The bond between the four of us was quite strong from the beginning. The community, however, was rather homogenous. The mixture of our races was out of place; as we became older it was impossible not to sense that most people found us a bit unnerving."

Nicci tried to break in, "Just because you . . ."

"Because," Madam interrupted, "we were *different* from the general population in town."

Mrs. Morph cracked her gum and leaned into the table. "As we got older, the kids made it hard on us—especially Marcus." Madam opened her mouth to speak, but Mrs. Morph was ahead of her. She addressed Madam rather strongly, "And don't you tell me to call him *Senator Whoozeewhatsee* 'cause I can't ever remember that goofy last name he's usin'." She focused on Mateo and his friends again. "His real first name is Marcus, and as we got older, he had it real tough. See, most everyone in that little town was white—like him. There wasn't anybody else in the school along the makings of yours truly," she said, fluffing her hair, "or the two of them either." She gestured toward Madam and the doctor.

"Our cultural mix," Madam continued, "was unacceptable both in the neighborhood and at school."

"But if this all happened before the Merger, then . . ." Dirk instinctively reached toward Madam's mind. He was not even conscious of the fact that he was jumping ahead and beginning to pull the information from her that he wanted to know.

"Mr. Tyrone," Madam looked sternly at Dirk. "I should greatly appreciate it if you would permit me to manage my own thoughts—and to expel them at my own rate."

Dirk snapped his mind back from hers. "Sorry," he said. "I didn't even realize . . ."

"Don't worry about it, kid," said Mrs. Morph, "It takes some gettin' used to, controlling these abilities we got. She knows you didn't mean it."

"As Mrs. Morph mentioned, the neighborhood and school community were made up of mostly Caucasians. The three of us were a rare phenomenon indeed, and as teens we were an easy target for persecution, both verbal and physical, I'm afraid." Madam spoke with regret.

"Most teens are insecure. They are searching for themselves. To persecute someone else gives them a heightened sense of security. It is a false sense of security, but it *feels* good," added Dr. Pan.

"Marcus," Madam was apparently going to use the Senator's first name now, "had offers to join the most popular crowds and teams, but he resisted. He refused to give up his allegiance to us, and it cost him all the way along. It cost him *dearly* in the end." Madam's tone became grave, and the air suddenly felt weighted.

Keiko sensed tremendous sorrow within each of the Elders. She knew, immediately, that whatever had happened to the Senator as a teenager had been life-changing . . . and terrible.

"Marcus defied the majority when he maintained his close relationship with us, and the majority doesn't generally like to be scorned." Dr. Pan shook his head in sorrow. "They turned on him when he refused to take part in their teams. When he was invited to parties—and we were not—he refused to go. They hated him for it."

"Them popular kids shouted nasty stuff at him in the halls, and they roughed him up sometimes. One time, the Doc here found Marcus in an alley where they had strung him up with some clothesline and spray painted him a whole buncha colors. They called him *The Rainbow Kid* after that on accounta he hung out with us. The paint job was a message, I guess you could say, that he wasn't choosin' the right friends. By the time Margie and me showed up, he was really worked up. I remember the look in his eye. Them kids had pushed him right to the edge." Mrs. Morph shook her head vigorously for a moment as if trying to shake the memory from her mind. Then, she took out her nail file and went to work.

"Eventually, that same group pushed Marcus *over* the edge," the doctor added as he glanced at the floor.

"They *killed* his father?" Dirk asked the question but already knew the answer because Dr. Panacea's thoughts were so open that Dirk had read them without meaning to.

"What?" Nicci raised her hand to her mouth.

"No—surely . . ." but Keiko did not finish the thought.

"Man, you gotta be kiddin'!" Mateo looked at Madam for confirmation, but it was the doctor who spoke.

"A few weeks after Marcus was *attacked,* he was given a chance to set things right with some of the athletes. The basketball team had nearly won the state tournament the preceding year, and most of the team's key players had another year left. Marcus was tall and very skilled—that was no secret. He was asked by the coach to play ball and help the team go all the way; Marcus flatly refused. He told the coach that until the school community welcomed *all* students and treated all students equally, he could not support the school."

"He was talkin' about *us,* ya know. *We* was the ones that weren't bein' welcomed. Things coulda been fine for him if he woulda cut ties with us!" Mrs. Morph was suddenly off her feet and quickly transforming into one outrageous creature after another. She was a blue guinea pig, a chartreuse duck, a purple orangutan, a crimson elephant, a green zebra— finally, she settled on a rather large pink poodle. She began talking a mile a minute and chomping her gum. "There I was in the ladies room—answerin' the call of Mother Nature 'cause that chili they served us at lunch was . . .".

"*Mrs. Morph* . . . to the point!" Madam's impatience was evident.

The poodle regarded Madam Moment for a brief moment, then placed its front paws on the table as it sat down very slowly. "Now, as I was sayin'—I was usin' the facilities when *Bambi Primrose* and them cheerleaders come in all *Rah! Rah!* like they do, and *then* I hear 'em sayin' that the basketball players are gonna get Marcus good for turnin' down coach's offer. Well, Bambi, she's just about to say what it is they're gonna do, when yours truly has a little moment that's not quite so delicate and ladylike—if ya know what I mean—and Bambi and her crowd skate right outta the bathroom, believe you me."

Madam, who was completely aghast at Mrs. Morph's casual manner, continued briskly. "We found Marcus immediately and told him that he was in danger, but he refused to hide from them. He didn't want to move around the community in fear, which was admirable, but we were concerned for his safety. We went to talk with him again that evening, but he wasn't home."

"So we told his parents everything," Dr. Pan confessed. "They knew there had been trouble for the four of us from time to time, but they had no idea how serious it had become. His father went to look for him immediately, and we stayed at the house and waited for them . . . until we heard the police sirens."

Doctor Pan's mind had remained open to Dirk—who was getting more of the story mentally than through the Elders' words. And it was Dirk, now, who told his friends the story's conclusion.

"They *stoned* him!" Dirk shuddered as he said the words. "He found the whole group of them beating the snot out of his kid, and he couldn't stop them. They . . . they started throwing stones at him . . . and his dad . . . and he shoved Marcus to the ground and covered him with his body. One of the rocks caught his head just right, and that was it. What a *stupid* way to die!" Dirk looked at Madam for confirmation, but she did not speak.

"Marcus was never the same again; after losing his pop, he decided to hate, too. In some ways, I couldn't blame the guy." Mrs. Morph reverted to her familiar form. "I remember—that was when he first started all that crazy talk—like looking different from one another really *was* a problem. It's funny how things change. I never woulda believed the guy who nearly lost his life protectin' us would betray us all in the end."

Madam stood. "The hour is late; the discussion has been heavy. Perhaps it has been enough for tonight."

"Actually, I'm not one bit tired," said Mateo with a yawn. "Guys like me, we can do the all-night thing whenever we need to—just say the word." He did not seem to notice that he was stretching both arms to the sky and yawning a second time while talking.

Dirk spoke respectfully to Madam. "I can't sleep, not yet. I need to know how you developed your powers."

CHAPTER 7

Mrs. Morph became quite excited. "Now that's a story worth tellin', eh, Margie? Come on—sit your booty back in the saddle there—she pointed to Madam's chair—and let *this* girl start things off!" Without waiting for a response, Mrs. Morph launched into her story, and, Dirk noted, Madam quietly seated herself at the table again. "Well, like we told ya, our folks was real brainy about science-type stuff—ya know DNA and RNA and biology and chemistry and—HEY! I made up a song once—outta them chemical symbols for the elements . . ."

Madam tapped her index finger against the table three times. "Mrs. Mooorrrrph! To the *issue* please!"

"Okay, okay!" Mrs. Morph grabbed for a new stick of gum, and Dr. Pan saw a window of opportunity to take over the story—almost. Just as he opened his mouth to speak, Mrs. Morph's eyes lit up, and she continued the tale in her typical spirited fashion. "Anyhow, all the scientists at the research lab, including our folks, got called in to study a bunch of mold somebody found growin' in the school. Whooeee! Them school board members and administrators was resignin' left and right! Teachers started gettin' sick—all kinda stuff! I had more study halls than classes that year, I'm here ta tell ya!" Mrs. Morph snorted and slapped her knees a few times.

"Did your abilities develop because of the mold in the school?" Keiko chided herself for interrupting, but she was worried Mrs. Morph would forget the reason for telling her story.

Dr. Pan responded, "No, child, it was not exposure in the *school* that brought us our powers. It was an accident, in some regards an ill-fated one, that manifested them."

"What happened?" Mateo shifted uneasily. He wondered if the *accident* had been painful.

"One afternoon, not long after the mold studies were underway, we decided to visit a section of the research laboratory that was off limits." Dr. Pan looked guilty even retelling the story. He reached for his stethoscope and patted it against his lab coat for comfort.

"Wow! If I'da known then . . ." began Mrs. Morph, but the doctor cut her off.

"I overheard my parents at dinner one evening," he said, "discussing the discovery of an old sewer pipe that led to a tunnel providing access into the restricted area of the lab. They agreed something was going to have to be done about it right away."

"Well, kiddos, that was all the information we needed to realize this was a great chance to take a looksee at what nobody else was gettin' to see. So, there I was, leading the way." Mrs. Morph had wrested control of the story from Dr. Pan again, but he was not to be outdone.

"I believe it was *I* who led the way!" he said in a corrective tone.

"It was *Marcus,* but that is beside the point," Madam interjected. "The point is that we were foolish to even consider going inside that laboratory. They had exposed the molds to a multitude of chemicals as part of their work, and bottles of the extract had been placed in the refrigerator."

"Well," Mrs. Morph chomped as she spoke. "I ain't quite the research-type, if ya know what I mean. So when I looked in the fridge and saw some bottles of soda, I said, 'Let's have us a little thirst quenchin' session.' Ya know? Who woulda thought a buncha scholars would go puttin' their fancy solutions in regular old soda bottles!"

"That was just the point! Anyone snooping about for information on their work would never assume the extracts in those bottles were anything more than beverages. We've been over this before—countless times." Madam sounded slightly exasperated and turned her attention back to the teens. "You are all quite personally familiar with the effects of our decision that day. You see, our parents were conducting experiments on the exposure of the molds to DNA samples . . ."

"And we drunk 'em up! I thought it was just flat soda—who woulda thought it would turn me into the gal ya got right here before ya!" Mrs. Morph's snorted in amazement and slapped her knee.

"Our abilities manifested themselves a short time after the death of Marcus' father," Dr. Pan began, but he was unable to finish as Mrs. Morph interceded.

"Boy, oh, boy! Marcus was furious when he started gettin' all those telepathic abilities. He saw it as just one more way of bein' different."

She stopped to breathe, and Dr. Pan took the lead from her. "Marcus didn't even want to *use* his powers at first. He preferred not even to discuss them, but he was forced to. Our parents drilled us night and day about keeping them a secret. They feared if anyone discovered our abilities, it would lead to all types of experiments on us. They were afraid we'd be taken away from them," he explained.

"But we were adolescents. We wanted to test our abilities, to learn their limits, and so we met each afternoon in a secluded glade not far from our homes. It was in those woods that we made the discovery that would eventually lead Marcus to betray us . . . and to create the Merger." The wistful look of remembrance faded quickly from Madam's face as she mentioned the Merger. It was clear to her young audience that the pain of the betrayal had not lost its potency over time.

Madam seemed to become lost in a memory again. "We had come together in a circle, arms spread across one another's shoulders, reciting some silly creed we'd made up about how we would remain friends for all time. That was the first time it happened. Marcus reached out and *joined* us to one another mentally."

"At first it was a strange, frightening feeling, but I sensed that and instinctively quieted everyone's fears. It was my pleasure, really, to make everyone feel more at ease," Dr. Pan beamed cheerfully.

"Ssssshhh! Ya gotta stop interruptin' Margie all the time, or I'm here to tell ya there's gonna be trouble. Why, I remember this one time when she was tryin' to explain . . ." Mateo touched Mrs. Morph's arm and nodded toward Madam who was clearly waiting to proceed. "Oops, heh! Heh! Sorry there, Margie. I got 'em all quieted down for ya, though."

"A tremendous confidence began to swell within us as we stood in that circle," Madam continued. "Through the joining of our minds, with Marcus as the conductor, we were able to understand on a much deeper level the most essential qualities of our friendship: loyalty, trust, sacrifice, and love. We truly understood in that moment all that words can never express about friendship, and we were strengthened by the knowledge of our devotion to one another—strengthened not only emotionally but physically." Madam looked at her young charges. "Following this joining or *merging* as we came to think of it, our powers were actually strengthened. We were emboldened, more confident than before. I believe the reassurance of the devotion of our friends permitted us to go where we might not have gone before. It was following this incident that I first carried all of them with me through time and felt no pain. Prior to that I had only taken one traveler with me, and the pain was nearly unbearable." Nicci nodded in silent understanding and felt comforted to know that Madam had not always found time travel as easy as she made it look today.

"And I was able to heal without physically touching whomever or whatever I was trying to aid," Dr. Pan added.

"It was marvelous to be able to heal from a distance." At his words Keiko felt both a pang of jealousy and a sense of hope—that she, too, would acquire this ability.

"What a hoot that was!" shouted Mrs. Morph, clearly remembering. "Suddenly, I could keep the shape, ya know, of whatever I was turnin' into—even when I got nervous. *That* was a biggie, I'm here to tell you! Used to be I would just go all to pieces when anything unexpected happened and then, well I couldn't hold a shape worth nothin'." She poked Mateo again. "You know what I mean, kid? But then, after Marcus did that old razzle-dazzle in the head thing, oh wow, I was a lean, mean, transformin' machine!" She looked at the teens as she chomped her gum excitedly, and Mateo grinned and nodded.

Dirk looked to Madam Moment. "So that's why your abilities are so much greater than ours—because he joined your minds that day in the woods?"

"Not just that day, Mr. Tyrone. Many days. You see, the confidence gained through this process was temporary. It lasted several days at first and for weeks later on, but it always dissipated after a time. We realized too late that instead of trying to grow confidence in our abilities on our own, we were relying exclusively on one another."

"No substitute for hard work, I always say," crowed Mrs. Morph. Dr. Pan and Madam Moment looked at her questioningly. "Well, I say that *now,* I mean. Geez! You people sure got some memory fibers working double-time over there. I'll admit it was pretty nice gettin' all my confidence from everybody else."

"We did not understand that depending so heavily on the group was keeping us from growing as individuals," Dr. Pan added. "I'm so sorry I did not realize it then. Things might have been different."

Madam continued, "Marcus was experiencing tremendous mental growth during these times as well, but his discontent with our community and the persecution we faced in school led him to a near obsession with racial intolerance. He read everything there was to read about it. It became the consistent focus in every paper he wrote. He scoured the newspapers and listened to radio and television—seizing the slightest story that smacked of racial persecution and learning all that he could about the details of it."

"He went a little loony upstairs if ya ask this girl right here, okay? I mean it got to be that the only thing he want-ed to talk about was how the world would be so much better if we were all basically the same. I mean, come on! If I had any idea he was as serious as he was, I'da been bowin' out of those head sessions of his right then and there!" said Mrs. Morph.

"Marcus became increasingly irritable when we did not agree with his suggestion that the world might be better off with only one race," Dr. Pan took over again. "I believe the conditions in our small town and the loss of his father truly began to affect the way he looked at the entire world. He generalized racial intolerance to be the world's one true evil, and he saw it everywhere—even where it was not truly present."

"One afternoon he asked us to meet him in the woods for a merging. We all looked forward to these times, and we arrived expecting it would be as it had always been. But this time, something was different. I sensed it as soon as I entered the woods." Madam grimaced as she continued the story. "Marcus asked us to sit down. He told us he had a pro-posal that he wanted us to consider. 'What if,' he proposed, 'people's racial differences could disappear? What if racial traits could be physically merged in the same way that we four were merging mentally?' He pointed out the tremen-dous harmony and confidence we felt during our sessions, as well as the aftermath, in which our abilities were strength-ened, as examples of how beneficial a merging could be."

"I thought that was just plain loopy and said as much! I

mean he was talkin' apples and oranges." This time Mrs. Morph elbowed Nicci. "I don't know if ya picked up on this honey, but I'm the kinda girl who just lays it all out there, ya know?"

"We expressed great reservations about Marcus' idea, and for the first time his anger became visible; he lashed out at us. He was enraged—screaming, calling us names, hurling accusations. His soul was deeply troubled. I could sense it, but sadly, the healing of the soul will always be beyond my reach." Keiko could identify Dr. Pan's regret as he spoke for she felt it herself, and she was only listening to the tale. "We left the glade that day, not as four but as three."

"Didn't he apologize or something?" Nicci questioned. "I mean the guy sure owed you some kind of . . ."

"The apology came, Miss Golden, and a request to meet again in the glade. Marcus rambled through a few words of regret, but they were clearly not heartfelt. He was distracted— that was quite evident. He was also *unusually* anxious to begin the merging. Something inside me felt that we should not join with him under these conditions; my abilities gave me a sense, quite literally, that the *time* was not right. But . . . I had come to rely on the group identity rather than trusting myself to do what I knew was right. I hold myself responsible." Madam looked directly into Nicci's eyes as she spoke now with frightening intensity. "I remained silent; I went along with the merging that day even though I knew it was wrong, and the world you were born into is the result of my silence."

CHAPTER 8

Dr. Pan broke in, "Madam, the responsibility is shared by *all* of us."

"Yeah, boy, I could hardly wait to get juiced up again by old Marcus. We all ignored the signs that something was wrong. You know we did, Margie. It wasn't only you." Mrs. Morph walked over to her colleague, and as she did so her form altered to that of a woman the teens had never seen before. The unfamiliar woman placed a hand on Madam's shoulder and spoke with a tone of loving authority, "Margaret, you must stop carrying the weight of the world on your shoulders. It is good to accept responsibility for mistakes when you make them. Your father and I are proud of you for doing so, but let's remember to allow others to do the same. It helps them grow up, and it will keep your heart a bit lighter."

A moment of silence passed as Madam regarded her friend thoughtfully. It was clear to everyone that the wise words, delivered by Mrs. Morph in the guise of Madam's own mother, were a reminder of a similar conversation when Madam was a girl. "Thank you, Mrs. Morph, we can all use reminders, and the past is a very good teacher . . . when we are willing to listen." She adjusted her robe, and Mrs. Morph returned to her seat, effortlessly assuming her usual appearance once again.

"The merging began on that fateful day as it always did with the four of us encircled," Madam continued the story that would reveal Marcus's betrayal. "We closed our eyes, as usual, to concentrate, relax, and allow Marcus to enter our minds and bring us together. Quite suddenly, though, I sensed something happening in physical time, outside of our merging, and opened my eyes to see two of my friends collapse silently to the ground. As they were standing on either side of Marcus, he was able to inject them with a solution that rendered them unconscious. He was unable to use the same technique on me, but it was not necessary. With both of them out of the way, Marcus knew that I alone would be no match for him. The gentle and respectful manner with which he had always inhabited my mind was abandoned as he assaulted me with such tremendous mental energy that I could hear myself crying out in physical time, but there was no one to hear me. Marcus could not keep his plan from me as our minds merged, nor did he need to. His considerable mental abilities were far more than I could resist."

Madam took a brief rest from the story just when it was about to climax, and Dirk found himself wondering if adults planned things this way. His patience was quickly rewarded, though, as she began to share the shocking details of the Senator's betrayal.

"When I say that Marcus *assaulted* me, assaulted all of us before the day was done, I am using a very carefully chosen word." Madam's voice became hard as stone. "He *stole* a portion of our abilities from us—took them against our will and left us with an emptiness that is impossible for you to imagine."

Keiko gasped audibly. The emotional pain, the betrayal, the assault, and finally the *emptiness* filled the room as the Elders relived the moment through Madam's words. Keiko leaned unconsciously into Dirk, who steadied her. He avoided the temptation to involve himself mentally in any part of what was going on. He heard the words but did not want to acknowledge what had happened. Madam was wrong. He *could* imagine the emptiness they'd been left with, the sense of violation they'd felt, and the realization, afterward, that the assault had come from one they called friend. He marveled at them. Today, there was no outward sign that they had ever endured such a terrible experience.

"Man! That guy is worse than scum. What kind of lowlife turns on his own friends?" Mateo was standing now and bursting with energy. *Sitting,* in this cave, listening to all these stories while the guy was out there, looking for them, *hunting* them, was crazy. *"Well, come on,"* Mateo thought. *"Come and get me!"* His transformation was impulsive, he knew, but somebody needed to *do* something. A throaty growl echoed through the cave, and Nicci screamed as a large grey wolf occupied the space where Mateo had been standing. It swung its head to the left, then right, bared its ferocious teeth, and headed toward the cave entrance. The creature looked back at them for a moment, then turned to go but found itself facing a much more omnipotent foe. A tiger, nearly twice the wolf's size, barred the entrance. It picked Mateo up, literally, and began speaking. "Hey there, puppy! I don't think you wanna mess with me, okee dokee? Goin' outside right now—it ain't such a good idea—ya know what I mean? So get your little self back over there with your friends before you *make my day!"*

The tiger released Mateo, who began falling from on high. He panicked on the descent, of course, and could not maintain the shape of the wolf. Despite his best effort, he reverted to his human form and landed unceremoniously on his rear. Nicci was unsuccessful in trying to stifle a giggle.

Mateo's eye's blazed. "You think it's funny, Nicci? Well, that dude is out there, somewhere, lookin' for us, and I don't see sittin' around here gettin' us anywhere. I say we go after him before he finds us. I say we . . ."

"Mr. Rodriguez, your passion is admirable, but in your present state you are hardly a match for Marcus. You will be seated again," Madam intoned. When he did not move, she responded with commanding authority, "NOW!"

Mrs. Morph, who was standing beside Mateo, whispered

in his ear. "I'd sit, kid, before she sends you somewhere that ain't so attractive. You check out sanitary conditions on the *Mayflower* sometime courtesy of this lady, and lemme tell ya, you won't be forgettin' to listen to her good sense. Them Pilgrims was a smelly bunch, and the *facilities* for bathroom breaks was, how shall we say, less than what you'd hope for on one of them extended voyages. I speak from experience on that one, kid, but you don't need to pass that around. If ya know what I mean."

Mateo sat.

Nicci tried to make peace with Mateo by refocusing the conversation. "So, what was the attack on you all about? You said Marcus stole a portion of your abilities, but why?"

"To bring about the world you see today," Madam replied. "My ability to travel into the past was severely limited by Marcus' attack. I can take only one companion with me if I travel backward in time. Since the attack, Marcus is able to move in and out of time at will. He cannot use time offensively, as I can, and he cannot take a companion with him through time—with one exception." The teens looked at her expectantly; however, her response was flat. "The exception is for another discussion."

Dr. Panacea began unbuttoning and rebuttoning his lab coat as he spoke. It seemed, to Dirk, that discussions about the Senator produced great anxiety in Dr. Pan. "Since Marcus' attack on us," the doctor said, "I have needed much greater time to pass between healings. It is as if I need to recharge, and that was not true before. Marcus cannot heal others, but because of what he stole from me, he can care for himself to a great extent. It saddens me to think that his first thought was of self-preservation."

"And listen to this," said Mrs. Morph. "He implanted something inside the old noggin here to keep me from assuming his form. I mean, I can do it for a few seconds— like I was showin' you kids earlier—but that's it. I suppose it was some kinda safeguard against me impersonatin' him. Like I'd ever want to *be* him! Since the attack, he's been able to become anything that suits his fancy, but he can't hold any shape other than his Sentor Broogue I.D. for more than a few minutes. And," Mrs. Morph fluffed her hair with both hands and smiled, "he ain't as *fast* as I am. I can tell you that, yes, sir!"

Long moments of silence followed. Keiko was flooded with a torrent of emotions, both from her friends and their older counterparts. Dr. Pan gestured toward her. "Madam, this one needs rest. It has been a long and difficult day." Keiko's eyes met those of Dr. Pan. He extended his hand in her direction and, instantaneously, she felt all of her worries, fears, and sorrow draining away; a soothing warmth began to restore her. "They are overwhelmed. Allow me to minister to them for a time."

Madam gave a small nod. "We are finished for today." She stood and faced Dirk and his friends. "Tomorrow, you will begin your *training*. We will serve as your mentors for there is much you need to learn . . . and time is short. There are somewhat crude accommodations deep within the recesses of this cave. Thus far they have shielded us from Marcus; however, now he has more reason to seek us than ever before. We must remain guarded at all times."

Dirk stood and his friends, with the exception of Keiko, followed suit. *"Training?* What do you mean training? You think you're going to enroll us in some kind of superhero boot camp or something? I mean thanks for saving us and all, but we . . ." With a flick of her wrist, Madam rendered Dirk immobile. He stood completely frozen with his jaw still forming the next word.

"The young are so impetuous." Madam regarded Dirk's companions. "I am sending the three of you to rest. Dr. Panacea will see to your needs. I will speak to Mr. Tyrone alone for a time, and he will rejoin you in the morning."

"Good idea, Margie. Ya know I was thinkin' you might want me to sit in on this talk with the kid and all because I kinda got a *way* with people. Ya know what I mean?"

Madam regarded her colleague with a hint of a twinkle in her eye. "Mrs. Morph, your kind offer is appreciated, but I shall decline. I would like you to stand the first watch around the cave's perimeter. I trust you shall find a form suitable for camouflaging yourself from Marcus' detection?"

Mrs. Morph clapped her hands. "Are you kiddin'? I gotta million of 'em." Mrs. Morph began assuming shapes in rapid succession. She was a giant squid, a firefly, a venus flytrap, some type of purple monstrous figure with a sparkling silver headband, and, finally, a great horned owl that took flight toward the entrance of the cave. Mateo was stunned, as always, at the speed of her transformations.

Dr. Pan extended a hand to Keiko, and they rose and went to stand with the others. "We are ready, Madam."

Madam looked tired, Nicci thought, as she gestured toward them and summoned her power to move them a few minutes into the future where they found themselves resting on makeshift beds in the lower tunnels of the cave.

" . . . can take care of ourselves, you know." Dirk completed the sentence he had begun before Madam froze him in time. Then, he looked around sheepishly. Everyone was gone except Madam, who was eyeing him with a trace of amusement. She patted a large boulder beside her. "Dirk," this was the first time she had used his first name, "come and sit a while." There was something different about her voice, Dirk noted. That tone that reminded him of a strict teacher, a commanding general . . . it was gone. She sounded almost grandmotherly.

He walked toward her, intrigued, but couldn't stop himself from commenting, "So are you going to blow a bugle and make us line up for you tomorrow morning?"

"It would be best, *Mr. Tyrone,* if you laid aside the sarcasm for a while. You are angry. You are grieving, and it is understandable, but you need to set your emotions aside for a time and listen. You and your friends are in grave danger; now that Marcus knows you are with us, he will search for you without ceasing."

"Why? Why does he care so much? I mean we've been living with Aunt Lisa in the shelter for years. No one's seen us. We haven't messed with his perfect little world, and I don't intend to. If we keep ourselves separate from the rest of society, how are we such a threat?"

"You are a threat because of what you can do. The four of you are the only ones in all the universe who could defeat Marcus and return the world to the way it was intended to be."

"How? We don't know anything about any of this. I'm not sure we even care."

"You *will* care, Dirk. And you will know everything because I shall tell you. And when I am done telling you, it will be clear why Marcus will use all the power at his disposal to defeat you. *You* are the one who presents the greatest threat to him."

"Because I have the same power that he does, you mean."

"That is, in part, correct. You do share his telepathic abilities, though yours are less advanced due to your lack of experience. But you must always remember that Marcus has a portion of the abilities the rest of us possess. That is what makes him so powerful. He cannot overcome the three of us together, which is why we tend to stay in close physical proximity. But even with our combined abilities, we are unable to defeat him. The power he stole from us makes him quite formidable, but you and your friends *could* ultimately defeat him. He knows that, and it was his hope to destroy you long before we were able to instruct you in how best to use your abilities."

"But why did you wait so long? What if he had caught us when we were younger? What would he have done if . . ."

"You were always under our protection, Dirk. Your aunt knew that. There was no need for you to learn of us until you were old enough to understand all of this."

"If you were protecting us—then why did he catch us a few days ago? Why did Aunt Lisa have to . . ." He stopped short of saying the word. Saying it made it true.

"As I explained, Marcus is very powerful. He has devoted himself to finding you since the day your aunt took you into hiding. Sometimes, Dirk, despite our best efforts, we fail. Of course we never meant for you to be captured, but Marcus is a clever foe. It does not matter how he distracted us and discovered you. What's done cannot be undone. It is to the future that we must look, and yet the solution is in the past. That is the mysterious thing about time."

"Huh?" Dirk did not understand what Madam had just said, nor did he feel like pretending he did.

"Dirk, the Merger was brought about by an incident in the past. You see, Marcus knew that he alone would not be powerful enough to literally alter civilization. He would need many powerful leaders, governments of nations, kings, queens, prime ministers, and presidents to endorse the concept of one race. To impact so many at once, he used my ability to travel back in time, and while he was there, he was able to alter the timeline. The resulting impact was the merged culture that you know today. As I explained before, since his attack on us, I am unable to take both of my companions back in time with me, and I cannot undo what he has done by myself. Marcus and I are able to sense one another's presence as we move through time if we are in close proximity. A part of his consciousness remains in the past to alert him to any interlopers, so my slightest attempt at interfering with what he has done would have no chance of success."

"Okay. So, if you guys can't go back, why don't you just . . ."

"*We* can't go back. But you and your friends can. And with my assistance, you will be able to arrive near the time of Marcus' tampering. If you can undo what he has done, the Merger will be reversed. All of the races—not just the four represented by our group here—but *every* race of the world will be restored again. The Merger created a blending of races. Characteristics of some ethnicities are more prominent than others, but each race is represented in some way. Marcus felt this was most important; it was his way of honoring the cultures."

"Honoring them while he was wiping them off the face of the planet? That's an interesting way to look at it," Dirk grimaced.

Madam looked lost in a memory. "Marcus wasn't always like this. As he allowed desperation and devotion to his ideas to take over and drive him to action, his thinking became twisted. I would say that somewhere, deep inside, guilt over his betrayal of us pushed him over the edge of reason. To embrace hatred for anything or anyone who threatens one's sense of what is right can allow a person to commit unspeakable acts. Marcus has become lost in just such a situation. Dirk, you *can* do this. I can teach Nichelle how to take all of you back with her in time. She *has* the ability."

Dirk could hardly believe his ears. This lady did *not* know Nicci. "I got bad news for you, lady. You have about as much chance of getting Nicci to take three passengers with her on a trip into the past as I had of coming out of that freeze you put on me a minute ago! She's always said she can't go into the past. She hates using her ability; of all of us, she's the one who avoids it the most. She says it hurts her, and that's when she's just moving around by herself."

"And she is correct. The sensation of time displacement causes physical discomfort, a great deal at first. But it eases. I will teach her—just as Dr. Pan and Mrs. Morph will teach

your other friends how to better manipulate their powers.
Over the next few days, we will work intensively at the task
of strengthening your friends' abilities. You have the potential to become remarkably powerful. Ironic, is it not? The
four of you are both Marcus' greatest fear and our greatest
hope."

"Look, I can't speak for the others, but as for me—I'm not
seeing this as being *my* problem. I mean, I don't like living
my life in hiding, but saving the world is not exactly something I was banking on in the career department."

"Mr. Tyrone." Dirk noted Madam's teacher voice was back
. . . and the first-name thing was evidently over for the
moment. "We are not talking about *saving* the world. We're
talking about *restoring* it to the way it was intended to be.
Your aunt spent her entire life trying to ensure that you and
your friends would survive so that you could set things right
again. Surely that must hold sway in your decision."

Her reference to his Aunt Lisa triggered something in
Dirk. He jumped up. "Oh, fine! You want to use the old guilt
complex on me. Adults are all alike. Why don't you just use
your *advanced* abilities, since they're so much further along
than ours are, and *make* us do what you want? That's what
it'll come to in the end, anyway. Won't it? We don't really
have a choice."

Madam stood to her full height. Her commanding presence threatened to overwhelm Dirk, but he did not shrink
back. After all, he was right, and he knew it. "*Choice* is not
something that will be taken from you nor forced upon you,
Mr. Tyrone. It fails to become choice when that happens. The
choice is yours."

"Good." Dirk said with an edge to his voice. He wasn't sure
why he was so angry at this woman, but he was. Who was
she to stand there in her lily-white robe and tell him what
he and his friends should do? She and her colleagues had let
them be captured. It was their fault his aunt was dead.

"Good! Because my choice is to say NO! And I think the others will follow my lead." No sooner had he said the words than the thought struck him—*why* did he think the others would follow him? And wasn't *he* the one saying he did not want to be a leader? It was all so messed up.

Madam remained poised. "Perhaps they will follow you. Only *time* will . . ." She stopped. Her face appeared flooded with alarm! "Marcus is here." Before Dirk could respond, he was caught up with Madam in what he now knew to be a shift in time. Suddenly, they were standing beside the unconscious form of Mrs. Morph. For an old lady, Dirk thought, Madam moved with surprising speed. She seemed relieved to find her friend's pulse and then, without warning, all three of them were were swept away again by Madam's incredible power.

They appeared with a burst of light in a meeting room with a table and chairs. The room was not unlike the one Dirk had been in earlier, except this one was much smaller—and there were only three chairs and a table. *"This is where the Elders usually meet,"* he thought. Torch light cast shadows on the wall; they were much deeper underground. Madam's voice was controlled but grave as she called out, "Doctor! Marcus is here! Mrs. Morph requires your attention."

Dr. Pan came rushing hurriedly from a corridor. He seemed quite nervous. "Where? Where is he? What's happened to her?" His hands were extended as he rushed forward and even before he touched her, Mrs. Morph began to shift uneasily, as if coming out of a drugged state.

"We must gather the others immediately and stay close together," Madam was talking more to herself. Dirk listened in on her thoughts at a distance. Even in the midst of chaos, she remained calm and logical—considering the situation from several angles before taking action. He wondered if this is what made her a good leader—someone her companions trusted to make the right choices.

Dirk was unprepared for the scream of terror that pene-
trated his mind before the rest of them heard it audibly.
"Madam, he's with Nicci!" Dirk shouted in alarm. He could
not imagine Madam Moment moving them faster through
time than she had done just seconds before, yet she must
have because it seemed to him, this time, that they literally
materialized into Nicci's room with no movement at all. And
there, bending over her, was the man Dirk knew as Senator
Broogue, the man the Elders called Marcus.

CHAPTER 9

Before Madam could intervene, Dirk's mind was hurtling forward. He could feel the Senator's formidable psychic ability overwhelming Nicci as she struggled feebly to avoid his suggestion. "Sleep . . . sleep . . . Miss Golden." It was being forced upon her, yet the voice in her mind was soothing and gentle. Dirk realized at once that the Senator's intent was to lull her into a restful state so that her body's vital organs could be easily shut down. He charged into the psychic bond full force.

"Nicci! Don't listen to him. Fight!" Now that Dirk knew something about their adversary's history, he had some idea at least of how to handle himself. He spoke directly into the Senator's mind, *"Okay, big guy, why don't you pick on somebody who knows how to play your game?"*

The Senator could no longer afford to give Nicci his full attention, which was exactly what Dirk wanted. The powerful leader fired back mentally at Dirk—keeping their exchange private. *"You are nothing more than a pitiful flea, boy. I could crush you with a mere whisp of my imagination."*

"If it was that easy, I wouldn't still be here," Dirk challenged. He could sense a sinister thought flickering through the Senator's mind.

"Remember that giant, boy? He never did have his dinner!" The creature began rising again in Dirk's mind—the same giant who had tried to devour him before—licked its lips and reached out to grab him again, but Dirk was ready this time. Instantly, he snatched a memory from the Senator's mind and within seconds the giant was surrounded by high school kids—laughing and taunting. "Hey, it's Marcus, The

Rainbow Kid!" one of them shouted. "Where's the rest of the troop, huh? You know, all your *multicolored* friends! Ha! Ha! Ha!" And as the group began to howl with laughter, the giant dissolved. Dirk knew it was terribly cruel, but he was fighting for survival, and he knew this memory would give him a fighting chance.

"You little BEAST!" The Senator raged aloud now, and as he turned his full physical and mental attention to Dirk, the connection with Nicci was severed—allowing Madam to whisk her younger counterpart and the others away. Dirk faced the Senator and shuddered despite himself. The man's cold eyes appeared to be fueled by hatred—almost as if they could ignite Dirk where he stood. Senator Broogue turned his head this way and that and spoke aloud with great satisfaction. "Well, Mr. Tyrone! My old colleague seems to have saved your friend, but she's miscalculated, as she so often does. And this time it's going to *cost* her. He grinned with sheer delight. "She's left you alone and unprotected . . . with a *very* worthy adversary."

The room began to fill then, quickly, with some type of green gaseous toxin. It poured from every crevice in the walls and floor. In less than a second, Dirk could no longer see the Senator clearly. The man was nothing more than an image behind the gas. Dirk dropped to his knees seeking oxygen and was startled by the sound of hissing. His eyes widened as from all around him immense snakes began to converge. "Ha! Ha! Ha! Ha!" The Senator's laugh was mocking him. "Never send a *boy* to deal with a man, Madam. Perhaps you'll learn that some day. Oh, that's right—this was your only chance. Pity that he was the best you could muster. Your expectations were obviously far too great."

Dirk lay prostrate on the floor now as the gas invaded his lungs. He could feel an immense snake winding around his legs, pulling them tightly together and beginning to squeeze as it made its way up his torso. Was it a python? An anaconda? He couldn't tell, and it seemed likely that he would never know. A part of him felt that this was all in his mind, that it *couldn't* be real, yet he was unable to gain enough mental control to fight it. Everything was happening too fast. Could the Senator's mind truly be this powerful?

"Ya know, Marcus baby, ya gotta get some new duds! I mean that gray outfit does *nothin'* for your complexion. Ya know what I mean? Now lay off the kiddo, before I have to remind you why you should." The loud crack of Mrs. Morph's gum coincided with the disappearance of both the gas and the snakes. Dirk sat up slowly and took a deep breath. The stale air of the cave was practically invigorating compared to the gas that had been suffocating him. He got to his feet and saw that both Madam and Dr. Pan stood alongside Mrs. Morph.

The doctor smiled warmly at Dirk. "It was all in your mind, Dirk. You will be fine."

"The *mind* can be a very *dangerous* place, Doctor." The Senator's voice was edged with ice. "It would be a shame if *you* came down with some type of psychiatric condition now, wouldn't it?"

For a brief instant, Dirk sensed panic in the mind of Dr. Pan. The awesomeness of the Senator's power was becoming quite clear.

"Marcus, do not waste time with idle threats. You know that the doctor is safe from your powers, as are the rest of us, as long as we are together."

"You will address me as *Senator Broogue!* That is my title within the Alliance; I have earned it. Names from the past hold no meaning. The past is *dead.*"

"The past *informs* the future, *Senator*—when we are wise enough to take notice." Madam spoke matter-of-factly and emphasized his title dubiously.

"Hey, you can call yourself whatever makes ya feel good! But let's leave the kiddos out of it. Haven't you trashed enough kids in your day?" Mrs. Morph stepped forward in what looked, to Dirk, to be a bit of a challenge.

Senator Broogue ignored her entirely and kept his eyes trained on Madam. "Don't think I'm unaware of what you intend to do. You want to send them back into the past—you want them to do what you can't do yourselves! IDIOTS! Why can't you see what I've created here? The Merger has brought racial harmony to the entire world. It is . . ."

"It is *manufactured,* Senator," Dr. Pan spoke politely. "It is as much an illusion as the things you create with your mind. The world was not meant to be this way. You have brought about something that is unnatural. We seek to . . . uuuhhhhhh!"

"Is *this* an illusion, Doctor?" Dirk sensed a brief attack on the doctor but could not figure out how the Senator had accomplished it. From the doctor's physical response, Dirk would liken it to a punch in the chest, yet it seemed to have taken place in the doctor's mind.

Mrs. Morph began to transform but shifted back to her usual appearance when the doctor called out, "No, it is fine. I am quite . . . recovered."

"Senator," Madam measured her words carefully, "our intention is quite clear—as is yours. Neither side is willing to relinquish . . ."

"Give me the boy!" The Senator suggested it, abruptly, as though a new idea had just occurred to him. Dirk fought the instinct to move behind the Elders.

"You can't seriously think for one moment that we'd consider such a thing," Madam responded with outrage.

"Margie, you got that first part right. He *can't* seriously *think* for a minute."

"I'll leave the others alone if you'll just give him to me. You can't train him. You can't even understand him! Only *I* know how he feels, how he thinks. *I* understand his abilities." The Senator's tone was imploring.

"You seek now to possess that which only moments ago you sought to destroy. This should not be." Dr. Pan spoke softly and shook his head in wonderment.

"There is no discussion. Your intent is transparent, Marcus. It appears you suddenly have a *use* for him—besides his destruction. We will never allow it!" Dirk knew, somehow, that Madam had used the Senator's real name on purpose this time. "When next we meet only *time* will tell. Until then, begone. We three shall not separate again now that you know of this place. Thus, there is no reason for you to come here. The young ones are under our protection."

The Senator pursed his lips for a brief moment before replying. "Very soon, though, they will be on their own—in the past, in *my* domain. And I shall bring them down, Madam. *Hard.* I shall destroy them, and there will be nothing you can do to keep me from it. Don't send them into the past." He turned to Dirk. "Don't do what they ask of you, boy. They'd send you all to your deaths to satisfy their own purposes. Don't *trust* them! Remember, boy, there are *two* sides to every story. Seek me out, and I'll tell you the other side. I'll tell you the *secrets* they're keeping from you. I'll show you how to use your abilities in ways you never dreamed possible."

"Enough of this!" Madam spoke with intimidating force. The Senator disappeared as a result of her outburst, but he communicated mentally to Dirk as he departed. *"Listen to me, boy. I was wrong to seek to destroy you. I see that now. Your abilities are greater than I realized. You have no cause to trust me after I threatened you, but you must understand the reason I attacked you. Let me explain it to you. Let me tell you the other side of the story. Then, you can make a decision about where your allegiance should lie. Move away from the rest of them, when Madam is distracted, and call to me with your mind. I shall come and take you to a place where we can talk. You will not be harmed, I assure you. And once you have heard my side of the story, you can make your own decisions. Trust your only living ancestor to tell you the truth."*

CHAPTER 10

The first rays of morning sun made jagged shadows as they cut through tree branches far outside the cave where Keiko and her friends had slept restlessly. The group had left before dawn to begin their training and had traversed a fair distance when Madam split them onto three sides of a hill. Their physical distance was not great enough to leave them open for an attack by the Senator, but it allowed them some degree of privacy during their training.

Dr. Panacea adjusted his lab coat and fumbled with his stethoscope awkwardly for a moment as Keiko knelt to inspect some wildflowers growing nearby. When she did not pluck the flowers from the earth, he smiled warmly. "A good decision—a good decision indeed."

"What?" Keiko thought she knew what he meant, but she wanted to hear him say it.

"The flowers, child. Respect for all living things is the first order of our business!" The doctor chuckled softly. "You know, Keiko, that our power to heal is linked in some way with the energy of all other living creatures—including our own human race. We have a bit of a reciprocal relationship, you could say." He paused for a moment and closed his eyes— seeming to concentrate. When he spoke again, his eyes remain closed. "Do you know that pain exists in these woods? Can you *feel* that there is a need for healing nearby?"

Keiko instinctively thought of her friends. She had always felt finely attuned to their physical and emotional states. For example, she could sense that they were all a bit insecure about the training, and she sensed grief for Lisa Tyrone pressed deep below the surface in all of them, especially

Dirk. She was puzzled. Did the doctor want her to attempt to ease her friends' discomfort? To Keiko, it seemed normal and healthy that they would feel as they did. "I'm not sure what you mean, Dr. Pan? My friends seem . . ."

"It is a *bird,* child, not one of your friends! A fledgling has fallen from its nest; one wing has been crushed. The mother is gone, and it is terribly frightened and in pain."

Keiko faced the doctor with a mixture of sadness and astonishment.

"How can you know this?" she said in wonder. She couldn't imagine sensing the baby bird on her own, and what would it matter if she could? Her empathic abilities had never reached beyond humans.

Dr. Pan walked behind her, placed his hands on her shoulders, and pointed her toward the forest. "You can know it as I do," he said. "But you must do what is especially difficult for one so young. You must empty yourself of every selfish thought. You must think only of the needs of others." He stretched her arms out perpendicular to her body and opened her palms. She felt the sun's warmth . . . so comforting. "Now," he said, "open yourself to *all* of life. Concentrate, Keiko, on the needs around you."

She felt a stirring within her. Yes. There was such a need for healing in the world, far beyond her friends and the space they inhabited. Rapidly, she began to feel terror, intense fear, someone was about to be killed . . . and wait, somewhere else there was hunger—children were hungry— children who hadn't eaten in days . . . and there was disease—devastating disease—and the man had no one to care for him . . . an animal was being attacked somewhere by a predator, the tearing of its flesh . . . "Oh, oh, no!" she cried.

Dr. Pan steadied her. He knew what had happened. He spoke gently but with authority. "Now, the *woods,* please. You must focus on the needs *only* in the woods. Then, you will not be so overwhelmed."

Keiko felt a rush of anger. How could he ask her to forget all that she had just opened herself to? Who would care for those others? Why should she open herself to their pain only to abandon them? She warred with respecting Dr. Pan, whom she had regarded as kindly until now, and arguing with him. Respect won out for the moment. She focused on the woods. Nothing. Several moments went by and still nothing. "I can't find the bird," she said sharply. "In fact, I can't sense *any* need in the woods." She turned to face him. "I have never been able to heal an animal, Doctor. That must be why . . ."

He turned her back around. "The woods. Try again."

Keiko crossed her arms stubbornly as she faced the forest. Dr. Pan reached around and extended her arms again. She made a halfhearted attempt and was about to turn back to him when he spoke. "Keiko, you are angry with me and confused by my decision to ignore the needs you first perceived far beyond the boundaries of these woods. Your anger is selfish. You cannot find the bird in the woods because you are reserving part of your attention for yourself."

"But . . ." She turned to face him but before she was halfway around, he turned her forcefully back as if she were a small child in need of correction.

"The woods, Keiko. The bird needs attention soon. It is weakening."

She faced the woods and retorted. "Then *you* should help it, Doctor. I don't know if I can find it in time, and even if I can, I cannot heal from a distance as you do. I need physical touch in order to heal."

"No. You do not. You only *think* that you do. Confidence is what you need. Now . . . find the bird." The doctor took out a small handkerchief and mopped his brow. Allowing the bird to suffer when it was in such close proximity was troubling him, and he had to consciously keep himself from healing it so that Keiko could do the work.

Several moments passed as nothing but the sounds of nature filled their ears. At last, Keiko's anger dissolved, and she began to perceive the fledgling. The perception came slowly—like the tiniest ripple that can be followed to its original source. The bird was indeed failing just as the doctor had explained. Her genuine desire to save it broke her concentration as she stepped forward to go in search of it. "Ohhhh, I need to *go* to it if there's any hope at all that I can heal it! Doctor, there isn't time for me to learn how to heal it from here. Another time. I will learn when the need is not so great."

"The need is always great, child. And everyone's need, every-*thing's* need, is relative one to the other. Remember this."

"You don't understand!" She was trembling. The serene manner with which she typically carried herself was replaced with inner turmoil as if serpents were coiling inside of her and threatening to burst forth. "I have to heal it *now*. If I do it my way, there's a chance of success. I just need to find it." With no further explanation, she burst toward the woods and did not look back. She would find the bird, heal it, and explain to the doctor that she would work very hard during his next lesson but that this time she simply had to do things her way.

It was dark in this part of the forest. Heavily leafed trees seemed to reach for one another from opposite ends of the woods, casting shadows in large pockets of her path. She heard the doctor calling to her and felt guilty, but she pressed on. Keiko was the least likely of all of her friends to ignore an authority figure, but the doctor did not understand that she knew best how to use her ability.

The darkness intensified. She heard hurried footsteps. Her mentor was gaining on her. She hesitated, felt for the bird again, and made a quick dash to her right. She was falling over a tree root before she could even express her surprise at its appearance. "Owwww!" she cried out painfully.

Instinctively, she touched the ankle, concentrated on the pain, and immediately it was relieved. Dr. Panacea grasped her elbow firmly and pulled her up. He glanced around nervously and spoke in a tone of great concern as he hurriedly guided her back toward their point of origin. "Madam would *not* want us this far out," he spoke in a clear tone of reprimand. "Impulsivity often leads to trouble, Keiko. You endangered us both by moving so far from the group. In addition, the bird has died."

"What? How? Why did you let that happen? You could have saved it. I don't understand how a healer could . . ."

"*You* could have saved it, child. And, oh, I wish that you had. If you rely on me, Keiko, you will never learn to push the envelope of your abilities. The fledgling would have died this morning for certain if we had not come to this area. Our opportunity to intervene was random. We were not successful today—a sad reality." Dr. Panacea frowned slightly. "As healers, we cannot take the burden of the world onto our shoulders lest we be completely drained. That is why, when you became sensitized to the needs of the world at large, I asked you to concentrate on only a small area—one greater than your own circle of friends but not so great as to overwhelm you."

Keiko took a few steps and leaned against a large, moss-covered boulder. She tried to sense the bird again and felt nothing where there had once been life. She stared at the ground in shame. "I'm sorry, Doctor."

He rearranged the tongue depressors in his pocket as he walked to her. Then, he lifted her chin with his hand. "It is all right. Lessons are sometimes painful. Now," he said as his eyes began to twinkle merrily, "there is a doe about to give birth not far from here. She has been carrying two fawns, and this is quite unusual. One of the fawns has been delivered successfully, but the second is giving her trouble. Perhaps you can help a bit! Come, I shall teach you."

She took his hand, a tangible offering of forgiveness, and stepped forward to continue her training.

"Now, Matty-boy, I'm gonna be straight with ya right from the start 'cause that's the kinda gal I am. Ya know what I mean?" Mrs. Morph cracked the trademark piece of gum—of which she seemed to have an endless supply—and adjusted a new pair of glasses with overly large purple frames. Mateo didn't think she needed the glasses, but he decided not to ask. He smirked good-naturedly as she paced around him looking quite uncomfortable. If he hadn't known better, he'd think she was about to have *the talk* with him. He decided to say as much.

"So what's the hold up? I already know about the birds and the bees. You don't have to look so nervous." When she did not respond with one of her customary wisecracks, he began shifting uneasily on his feet.

She walked up, grabbed his ear roughly, and pulled his head down to her four-foot-eight-inch frame.

"Yowww!" Mateo grimaced, but she held him in place.

"Don't mess with me this morning, kid. I'm the *teacher,* you got that? You readin' me on this one, Matty-boy? In my family there was always this one thing—*Respect the teacher!* Pop said it from day one." She let loose of his ear. "And when Pop talked to us, the way I'm talking to you now, we listened!

"On the first day of kindergarten, Pop said to me, 'Minerva Jean, you *always* respect the teacher. The teachers; they love kids. They work hard to help you. I don't ever wanna hear my girl got in trouble with the teacher! You got that? Because if you get in trouble with the teacher—I tell you what—in *this* house, nobody's gonna be interested in your side of the story. You hear me, Minerva Jean?'" She elbowed Mateo. "When Pop called your names together like that, you knew it was serious stuff."

Mateo nearly burst out in laughter when Mrs. Morph

revealed her first name but managed to contain himself out of fear. He also thought of mentioning that using your kid's middle name to emphasize the significance of a conversation was a trend in world-wide parenting and no big revelation, but his ear was still smarting.

"Me. I'm not the kind to *teach,* ya know? I'm feelin' a little insecure and all, and I'm admittin' it right from the start. But if we're gonna get through this, you gotta respect the teach. You with me on this? *I'm* the teach. The *Teach.* I kinda like that. You call me that, Matty. You call me *Teach,* okay?" She rolled her shoulders forward a bit as if she were trying it on and smiled at him. "But you say it with respect."

"Er . . . sure. I guess."

She gave him what could only be described as "the look" all teachers know how to give when students have not responded correctly.

"I mean, yes, Ma'am," Mateo said quickly.

She folded her arms, continued to stare at him, and began tapping her foot impatiently.

Finally, he got it. "I mean, yes, *Teach,*" he said resolutely.

Throughout the morning Mrs. Morph proved to be a far better teacher than either she or Mateo would have predicted. Mateo liked the fact that she was prone to actually *do,* herself, the very kinds of transformations she expected of him. There was not a lot of talk in Mrs. Morph's class—just a lot of action.

"Matty-boy, we gotta work on speed. I mean pardon me for bein' blunt, kid, but you're like an old lady. And stop lettin' me see what you're gonna become! That's no good. I can see it in your eyes in advance. Never give away your secrets, Matty," Mrs. Morph coached.

"But my friends think it's cool that my eyes reveal what I'm about to become," Mateo argued. He ignored her comment about his lack of speed because she was right. Compared to her, he was a snail.

"Become something!" she directed.

"Huh? What? Why should . . ."

"The correct response to my direction, Matty, is 'Yes, Teach.'"

He sighed. "Yes, Teach." The vision of a fly appeared in his eyes and just as he transfigured, Mrs. Morph became a spider who had him sewn into a web in the blink of an eye. He changed back immediately. "Hey! What's the big idea? You should have . . . "

"I *saw* what you were becoming and did you one better." She cracked her gum loudly— much to Mateo's annoyance.

"Well, most people aren't you. They aren't going to know to watch my eyes, and they don't have your abilities so . . ."

"Marcus." Her voice was as commanding as Mateo had ever heard it. "He knows, Matty. He will look for every advantage, and he'll use it." She walked over and patted Mateo's cheek. "I just want you to be safe, kid. Okay? The eye magic—it has to go."

Mateo was struck by her sensitivity. It seemed in that moment that her concern for him was more than was justified for someone he'd met only recently. "Sure, Teach." He responded. "I'll try."

"And I'll teach ya, kid! It ain't so much, really. My eyes used to do it, too. Still do, in fact, it's just I'm so fast that nobody can see the image. Now, let me show you how to pick up a little speed!"

Mateo gave Mrs. Morph his full attention for the rest of the day's training session, but the earlier moment of tenderness was never far from his mind. It eased the grief he was trying to bury over Lisa Tyrone's death, and it made him wonder if Mrs. Morph had ever had a child of her own.

Nicci Golden was beginning to feel a level of comfort with her unique ability to manipulate time. Using her power, even talking about it, had produced anxiety in her for as far back as she could remember. With Madam, though, it was different. The woman inspired confidence in Nicci. "She's *regal*," Nicci thought, "and powerful." Such a commanding presence was Madam Moment that Nicci found herself driven to please the woman and spent nearly the entire morning attempting to do so. She wanted Madam to think well of her.

"Miss Golden," Madam stated with a touch of pride in her voice. "You have made remarkable progress throughout this morning. You are to be commended!"

"So commend me, already," Nicci thought to herself. Madam was not given to emotional statements, though. Praise was doled out in a way that kept Nicci always at a distance. The warmth so evident in Dr. Pan and Mrs. Morph seemed buried somewhere inside Nicci's mentor. One could ask or one could wonder why Madam remained so reserved. Nicci regarded her mentor carefully but did not speak. For now, she would be satisfied with wondering.

"I believe," Madam said adjusting her robe, "that there is time for one last exercise. Miss Golden, I am going to attempt to send you away from this place—whether to the future or to the past is inconsequential—what *is* of consequence is that you are to keep me from doing so."

"What?" Nicci was thoroughly confused. "Madam, my ability is to move *through* time, not to hold it steady."

"You will remember, my dear, our meeting with the Senator and his men at the facility where you were being held. You saw me there, holding time constant. It can be done but with a much greater degree of concentration. Focus, Miss Golden, on holding back the past while simultaneously refusing to allow the future to move forward. I am asking only that you hold time constant for yourself, while I attempt to dislodge you."

And without further warning, before Nicci could even fully comply with Madam's instructions, she felt the inexorable tug of a shift in time. Madam was trying to pull her into the past. Nicci's lack of panic surprised even her. She remained calm and followed Madam's instructions to the letter. And as the attempt to displace her began to meet with a resistance that she herself was creating, Nicci's confidence took another giant step forward. Madam relented eventually and smiled the most genuine smile Nicci had seen to date. The woman made her way quickly to her protégé and placed her hands on the girl's shoulders. "Bravo! Miss Golden. That was quite remarkable."

"Well, you just bring out the best in me I guess," Nicci burst forth with praise before she could stop herself.

"Yes . . . well . . . I am pleased that my instruction is serving as an encouragement." The awkwardness lasted only a moment, but Nicci chided herself. Madam was clearly uncomfortable with receiving compliments.

"In the future, Miss Golden, the immediate future that is, I shall work on teaching you to use your abilities offensively rather than defensively. They will need to broaden in scope, and you must learn to travel through time with a larger number of people accompanying you."

Nicci tensed involuntarily at the mention of taking *passengers* with her.

"It is not a painful process, Miss Golden. Your *fear* has made you a prisoner. I shall release you."

"Madam, I don't know if I can. I've always been so . . ."

"It is not open to discussion. You *must* learn to do it, and so you *will*. Very soon you and your friends will be journeying together to someplace that even I have not traveled to in the company of others. You, and only you, will be able to bring them home again."

irk spent the entire morning watching, from a distance, as Madam Moment worked to broaden the scope of Nicci's abilities. He had been interested for the first hour or so, but he couldn't hear much at the distance Madam required he maintain from them, so his attention had turned to other things. The Senator's parting words were imbedded in his mind. He had been replaying them nearly all morning . . . word for word:

"Don't do what they ask of you, boy. They'd send you all to your deaths to satisfy their own purposes. Don't trust them!" What purposes was the Senator speaking of? The more Dirk thought about it, the more he began to question. True— Madam and her friends had saved them from the Senator— but did that make them trustworthy? What if they had saved them only to *use* them for some purpose of their own? It seemed, to Dirk anyway, that there were too many secrets. "And trust," he said aloud, "isn't built on secrets."

"Remember, boy, there are two sides to every story. Seek me out, and I'll tell you the other side. I'll tell you the secrets they're keeping from you. I'll show you how to use your abilities in ways you never dreamed possible." It was true. Dirk had always been told to remember that every story has two sides—and sometimes more than two. What would it hurt, he wondered, to know the other side? And what of *his* abilities? The others were receiving training from the Elders, but there was no one to help him. None of them could truly understand him. They didn't know what it was to wrestle with the incredible psychic energy that manifested itself within him. No. Only one other person could understand that.

Dirk was no fool; every encounter with the Senator had nearly cost him his life. If he was going to question the trustworthiness of Madam and her colleagues, then he certainly had to acknowledge that the Senator had shown himself to be far less than trustworthy. He was, in fact, a deadly enemy. And yet, Dirk was intrigued. He didn't think for a minute that the Senator intended to help him learn to more effectively use his abilities, but perhaps Dirk could glean something from a conversation with him that could be useful. Certainly hearing the other side of the story would give him something to question Madam and the others about. If nothing else, it might push them to be more honest with Dirk and his friends.

"You will not be harmed, I assure you." Dirk wasn't so sure about that, and yet he wanted to know more. He also had some idea, at this point, of the kind of attacks the Senator was likely to direct at him, and Dirk had formed some countermeasures in his mind. If there was any hope of answers to his questions, any hope of learning more about his abilities, Dirk knew the answers would have to come from the Senator.

"Trust your only living ancestor, Dirk, to tell you the truth." Was the Senator *truly* his ancestor? It would make sense—after all, Dirk and his friends *were* born with their abilities. This meant their powers had to have been passed down genetically. Was the Senator some kind of great, great-grandfather? With a start, Dirk realized that he had no way of knowing how old the Senator, or any of the Elders for that matter, truly were. The Elders' abilities could easily affect their longevity and appearance, and the Senator had all of their abilities—to some extent.

He moved in a bit closer toward Nicci and Madam Moment—just enough so that he could hear them. It sounded as though Madam was asking Nicci to attack her, offensively, by throwing her into another time period. If ever there was a time to escape Madam's notice, it would be now. Dirk took a deep breath and began to run. As soon as he felt confident that he was out of her range of protection, it would be time to call for the Senator.

Senator Broogue paced at the foot of the dais in the Great Hall of the Legion for World Alliance. He had remained in isolation the majority of the time since Madam and the others had defeated him in the cave. No one knew what was troubling him, nor could they be told. The fact that Dirk and his friends posed a tremendous threat to their society would be lost on all but the Senator's closest associates. And while a few of his colleagues were aware of the teen's existence, none of them knew of the supernatural abilities Dirk and his friends possessed, nor of the Senator's own unique abilities.

He had overseen the crafting of the Merger with great care. *Michael* had been the key. And as the Senator thought of the boy whose life he had saved, he was struck again by the awesomeness of the power of one. The potential a single individual had to shape the future lay dormant in most people—never fully realized or exercised in any tangible way. But sprinkled throughout history were a *few* people with vision—people with passion and a hope so extraordinary that the destiny of the world would be forever changed by their words and actions.

Michael Quinn had been such a person. Had his life ended, as it should have late one April evening, the world would have remained unchanged. But the Senator, combining his mental powers with the time-shifting abilities he had acquired from Madam Moment, had learned to see *alternate* timelines. He had spent years playing *what if* with time, searching for a moment he could alter that would make the world ripe for his vision of a society that was racially merged. There would be no more hate crimes, no more unjust hiring practices, no more taunting and teasing of children on playgrounds or in high school locker rooms. Merging the races would bring equality and a sense of brotherhood that would lead, the Senator was sure, to other benefits.

Why, there was no end to the harmony that could be created! And over the years, he had become so convinced of his mission, so passionate about the need for what he had termed the Merger, that little else mattered; he had become a man obsessed. And then one day, traveling into the past with his mind focused, as always, on identifying someone who represented a pivotal moment in time, he had discovered Michael Quinn. And he had known in an instant that the merging of every race on the planet could become a reality.

The Senator stepped to the large seat reserved for him on the dais of the Great Hall. He had never planned to become the most powerful figure on the planet; it had simply happened out of necessity. Once Michael's life had been spared, the Senator had needed to be present to manipulate the thinking of many key government leaders. Over the years, he had tended to all of the significant decision makers in the world, from Michael's time to the present day, just as a mother hen looks after her chicks. By the time the Merger was enacted, and the knowledge that there had ever been any division of race altered both historically and in the minds of the people, the Senator found himself a very influential person. In order to stabilize the Merger and ensure its longevity, it was necessary for him to retain a position of great power within the Alliance.

And of course there was the threat posed by Dirk and his friends. The Senator remembered all too well the day the call had come from the hospital. Dr. Lisa Tyrone, one of the leading geneticists employed by the Alliance, had sent a priority message, specifically to him. Four infants—born within a few hours of one another—appeared to have unique racial characteristics. Such a situation had never occurred since the Merger had been in place.

Standing in the hospital room that same day, looking at four tiny infants with features so different from one another, the Senator was reminded of those he had once called friends. Then, Lisa Tyrone had unexpectedly handed him the little Asian girl. There had been no chance to object. The doctor had bolted down the hallway to an emergency—leaving him stranded with the tiny cooing infant. And looking into that baby girl's almond-shaped eyes, he had weakened. She reminded him of a young boy he had grown up with—a boy he had known well. The boy had eyes and skin just like hers; he was of Asian descent. Suddenly, the Senator's mind had taken him into a memory he had buried long ago. He was in a dark alley—bloodied and broken, crying and alone. He had been beaten for defending his friends—none of whom were Caucasian as he was. It was unacceptable, to many in his high school community, that he allowed his friendship to cross racial boundaries, and so they had decided to "teach him a lesson he'd remember." The Asian boy had been the first of his friends to find him that night and comfort him. They had sat together all evening—talking of justice and injustice.

The Senator was startled from his memory at the realization, for the first time, of the significance that particular night held; the idea of a society void of any outward racial characteristics had settled on the perimeter of his consciousness that evening. The seed had been planted, the seed that would ultimately create the Merger . . . and bring the boys' friendship to a bitter end.

Awash in the painful memories, flames of *guilt* had licked at the Senator's insides. He was distracted by emotions and not as alert as he should have been to the fact that these were more than just innocent babes. His mental probe of them revealed a trace of their abilities, and he was suspicious at once. But he was also overwhelmed with a desire to get away from them—as quickly as he could—to escape the agonizing memory of his betrayal of his friends. When Lisa Tyrone had begged him for a chance to try to merge the infants, he had hurriedly granted her a few days and rushed from the facility. He had been running, in fact, when he left the building. Running from thoughts and feelings associated with his own painful past.

He should have destroyed the infants the minute he sensed their abilities! The mistake had eaten away at him for the past fifteen years. When the merging was unsuccessful, Dr. Tyrone had taken her nephew and the others into hiding to spare their lives. She had not known of their abilities at first, of course, but he was certain that Madam and her colleagues had come to her early on and revealed everything. The three of them, along with Dr. Tyrone, devoted themselves to protecting the four infants. They alone knew that these four had the power to reverse all that the Senator had done . . . and destroy the Merger.

"Senator Broogue," Dirk's mind spoke with urgency, *"I have moved away from the others, and they haven't noticed that I'm gone. You said there was another side of the story. Well, I'm ready to hear it."*

The Senator pushed away the painful memories, and his eyes lit up. "So, the fly has decided to step into the spider's web!" He blocked the thought even as he spoke the words aloud so that the boy would not sense the danger. Senator Broogue rubbed his hands together with anticipation. Initially, his plan had been to simply destroy Dirk as quickly as possible, but that was before he realized the extent of the boy's power. Now a new thought had taken root. If he could harness that power, siphon it from Dirk as he did from his friends so long ago, his own mental abilities would become unimaginable.

There was no end to the possibilities of what he could accomplish, to the good he could do for the world by adding Dirk's power to his own. The Elders and Dirk's young friends would no longer be of any consequence; their collective power would pale in comparison to his might. Dirk would resist, of course, and be little more than a vegetable when the Senator was finished with him, but that was the way of things. The Senator had learned there were always sacrifices where the greater good was involved. Dirk was about to learn it as well.

"Stay right where you are, boy. I shall be with you soon."

CHAPTER 12

The Senator appeared next to Dirk with all the speed and skill of Madam herself. He did not, however, whisk Dirk away in a shift of time as the boy had anticipated. Instead, he grabbed Dirk's arm and shoved him forward forcefully. "Move, boy, quickly! We must go *much* farther from here if I am to share with you all that you are eager to hear."

Dirk bolted forward followed by an overly eager Senator Broogue. "Can't you just transport us somewhere so we can talk?" Dirk questioned.

"My abilities do not allow me the luxury of taking a companion along in my travels through time," the Senator replied. It was a lie, of course. There was *one* person the Senator could transport through time with him, but that was not something he wanted Dirk to know.

"Maybe that's because you *stole* them from Madam. And the others, too." Dirk continued moving quickly. "They told me about your so-called friendship. No big surprise you're a traitor as well as a killer."

"There! Up the hill and toward that recessed area." The Senator pointed at what looked to Dirk like little more than a crevice in the hillside they were approaching. "My former colleagues have presented *a* truth to you, my boy; whether or not it is *the* truth remains to be seen. You shall know much more than you do now as soon as we secure our safety." The Senator grunted and pulled himself up an embankment. He was not used to such a physical mode of travel, but he could not afford to transport himself and leave the boy unattended. Not when he was so close to capturing him.

A few minutes later they were safely hidden in a decent-sized cave set back into the hill. A good hiding place, Dirk thought, as it was barely noticeable until you were quite close. "Okay," he spoke with a sense of authority he neither possessed nor truly felt, "let's hear this story you're dying to tell me."

The Senator moved quickly to Dirk's side and gestured for them to sit. "Not just yet, boy. First, we'll have to deal with my time-traveling old friend. She would not want you to hear what I'm about to tell you. In fact, she would stop at nothing to keep you and your friends from discovering the truth and the *danger* to which you will all soon be exposed. And Keiko Tan's life will be placed at risk . . . if they are allowed to proceed with their plans." The Senator had probed delicately enough to sense Dirk's strong feelings for Keiko. Playing on them, he hoped, would solidify the boy's willingness to proceed with the next step.

"I'm *not* going to hurt Madam Moment, if that's what you're thinking!" Dirk started to rise, but the Senator grasped his arm with great strength and pulled him back down. The man spoke in a whispered tone that was both desperate and harsh, and he never loosened his grip on Dirk. "We *must* immobilize her if I am to have time to explain what she is keeping from you. And then, there is the training I can offer—if you are interested. I think you will be once you hear the whole story, Dirk." It was the first time he had called the boy by name. He had been waiting, planning to use it at precisely the right moment to begin establishing a bond.

Dirk moved to stand, and the Senator released him. As he stepped out of the shadowy cave and back into the light just outside, Dirk realized that his uncertainty about meeting with the Senator alone was growing rapidly. He turned and walked back inside. "Start talking, Senator. I don't betray my friends. You can take the time you've got, or I'm outta here."

Senator Broogue quickly came to his feet. "You impudent
. . ." He stopped himself from saying any more and suppressed his rage. He walked quickly to where Dirk stood and
gently pulled him farther back into the shadows. "I've told
you, *Madam* will interfere. She'll likely arrive any minute if
we don't stop her." He assumed a conspiratorial tone. "We
needn't harm her, Dirk. We simply need her to rest for a
while . . . so that you have the chance to know her secrets.
Come now, you're a very powerful young man—you'll be able
to sense if I am trying to harm her. I give you my word, Dirk;
I shall do neither of you the least bit of harm. Besides, how
could you ever forgive yourself if what I'm going to tell you
could save Miss Tan's life? Didn't mean to probe, but it's
hard to miss such strong feelings. You know how it is."

Dirk thought of Keiko, so serene and trusting. If Madam
and her friends were planning to endanger her, he had to
know. He whirled to face the Senator with anger bubbling
inside. Was he a pawn in a game—playing right into the
Senator's hands, or was there some level of truth in the
man's words? He did not know. "I'm trusting you not to harm
anyone! We may be enemies, but this is a truce right now, so
we can talk. I assume you have *some* sense of honor."

The Senator's greed threatened to overwhelm him. He
had the boy! He was just moments away from securing the
Merger forever and doubling the power he possessed, if he
could just remain calm. Nothing too fast. "Don't scare him
and *don't* let him get a window into your thoughts," the
Senator told himself.

"In this, I am an *honorable* man, Dirk. Come and sit
again. We shall need to work together in order to persuade
Madam to sleep for a short time."

Dirk halted his approach and his mind leapt to an
extremely sensitive stage of alert. He was not about to willingly allow the Senator access to his mind—if that's what the
man was suggesting. Even entering Madam's consciousness

at the same time the Senator would be inhabiting it would be dangerous. "You're powerful enough to force her to sleep without me. I can just *tune in* to be certain you're not harming her." Dirk was pleased with himself for thinking of this. He felt like he was gaining control of the situation. Yes, he was in charge. He'd call the shots. "Go ahead, Senator," he issued the directive with authority he did not possess.

The Senator's face did not betray his annoyance. The boy continued to surprise him. Though he was foolish enough to separate himself from the group, he remained suspicious and alert. If the Senator tried to overtake him now, the boy would alert Madam, and his plan would fail. He steeled himself. "It's the *distance,* Dirk. She's quite powerful, you know. From this distance and with many other things taking place in the Alliance right now, my abilities are a bit tapped. I'll need your help to make it happen."

Dirk did not move. He was trying to sense deceit in the Senator's words but could find nothing to give him any sense of whether the man was being truthful at this exact moment. His mind was an impenetrable fortress.

"You either trust me, or you don't, Dirk. You've come this far. I am powerful and skilled, true, but also old and somewhat tired. You, on the other hand, are young and fresh . . . and also quite powerful. Surely you can protect yourself, though I assure you it will not be necessary." Dirk stared into the Senator's eyes, but he did not move nor did he speak. Suddenly, he knew. He should not have come here; this situation was far more dangerous than he had anticipated. He knew, too, that he was about to give in to the Senator's request.

Madam looked to the spot where Dirk had been observing them, and Nicci's eyes followed hers. Dirk was nowhere to be seen. A knot of fear formed in Nicci's stomach as she saw the strength of Madam's features, always so reliable and

assured, give way to what could only be described as terror.
The woman appeared about to speak when her hands moved
to her temples. She let out a soft moan, then collapsed without warning at Nicci's feet and did not move again.

Keiko and Dr. Pan were making their way back to the
point where the three groups had split off that morning.
Though the day had begun with difficulty, it had progressed
in a more positive fashion, and Keiko's confidence had grown.
She was eager for all that Dr. Pan would teach her in the
days that followed. As she moved to admire a patch of violets
along the path, Keiko suddenly stopped without warning.
"What is it, child?" Dr. Pan's voice queried.
"Dirk," she said curiously. "We share kind of a mental
bond. I can't exactly explain it, Doctor, but, well, we're very
close. He left a part of himself inside my mind. I can't read
his thoughts or anything, but I can feel his emotional state
at all times. He's feeling very conflicted right now. Ohhhh!"
She turned and pressed her back against a tree for support.
"There is regret. Tremendous regret. He has made a terrible
mistake. And someone is . . ."
Dr. Panacea felt the pain emanating from inside Keiko
before he heard her cry aloud. "Child!"
Keiko's body began sliding down to the base of the tree.
She was trying to protect herself from the mental assault,
trying to hold onto the link she shared with Dirk.
"Aaaaahhhhhh! He's there, Doctor! The Senator is *inside*
Dirk's . . . aaaahhhhhh! STOP! STOP! PLEEEEASE!"
"Madam! MADAM!" Dr. Panacea's mind raced with confu-
sion as he tried to summon Madam Moment to his side. But
where was his friend? Why had she not come instantly when
he called?
"AAAAAAAaaaaaaaaaaah! NO, DON'T! DON'T!" Keiko
was screeching and pressing her hands to her forehead.
Dr. Panacea placed his hands to each side of her head and

closed his eyes. He did not need the physical contact to help her, but it would likely be reassuring. Instantly, he began to pull the pain the Senator was creating in Keiko's mind away from her and into himself. The doctor winced and fought down panic as the Senator's attack passed into his own mind. Though he was an accomplished healer, dealing with the Senator was never a simple matter. Keiko was safe now, but Dr. Pan's body trembled visibly as he fought to ease his own suffering and dispel the agony left from the Senator's attack. At last, he was successful. The doctor took only the slightest moment to congratulate himself before kneeling gently beside Keiko. "Child!" he spoke with concern as a lone tear made its way down her cheek, "What is it? What has happened?"

"It's *Dirk*," she barely whispered the name. "He's gone."

"Now that's the way ta do it, kid! Ya know what I mean?" A giant bear gave Mateo a congratulatory slap on the back that sent him sprawling to the ground. "Oops! Sorry, there, kid." The bear transformed into Mrs. Morph as Mateo picked himself up off the ground for what seemed like the hundredth time that day. Mrs. Morph had a tendency to congratulate her student a little too often, and Mateo found himself wishing she would remember not to do so when she was a dragon, an elephant, or a bear. Still, he grinned as he walked back to her.

"No eyes?" he asked.

"I didn't see nothin' in them gorgeous brown eyes except my own reflection, kid! You was great. Ya know, if you was in school—the girls'd be chasin' ya down the halls and pretendin' ta drop all their books, Matty. I bet the girls'd really go for ya if ya'd had the chance to meet any of them. It's too bad you kiddos have spent your whole lives hidin' from Marcus."

Mateo blushed. "Aahhh, I don't know." He sat down on a

tree stump and pretended to study the ground.

Mrs. Morph came over and knelt beside him. The fragrance of nearby pines came to them on the wind. "Matty, I tell ya, the ladies'd love a guy like you! I mean you're a bee-you-tee-ful person!"

Mateo couldn't help but laugh. He shook his head from side to side and regarded her with affection. She was so sincere, almost like a mother. "It's *handsome,* Teach. You don't tell guys they're beautiful. You're supposed to say I'm *handsome.*"

She reached over and pinched his cheek. "Kid, nobody knows better than me how to turn a phrase. I been thinkin' about becomin' a poet, ya know? But, trust me—you *are* bee-you-tee-ful, and I'm talkin' about the inside, too, Matty-boy."

"Madam! MADAM!" The alarm in Dr. Pan's voice was unmistakable and the volume made it clear that something was very wrong.

The response from the metamorphs to the cry of their friend was immediate. The two human figures began to run and in mid-stride both were replaced by cheetahs, moving with great agility and with teeth bared.

CHAPTER 13

The Senator's plan was working perfectly; the attack against Madam had come without warning and had been entirely successful. Working together, he and Dirk had placed such a strong suggestion of sleep in her mind that she did not even move through the typical stages one experiences when resting for a lengthy period of time. Instead, her mind, aided by two others, brought the brain to rest in such a way that REM sleep occurred instantly. The Senator had purposely intended nothing more and allowed Dirk free access to his thoughts regarding the plan to render Madam inoperative for a time. This was necessary to build the boy's trust and encourage him to let down his guard.

Still, the Senator could feel his prey's sharp mind remaining somewhat alert to danger, and he was forced to admit that Dirk was not entirely naïve. But the boy was *not* skilled in the fine art of deception. He could never have anticipated that, initially, it was a *physical* assault the Senator was planning against him. As Madam drifted into a deep sleep, the Senator and Dirk began to extract their minds from hers, and without the slightest warning the Senator struck! He plunged a needle into Dirk's neck with tremendous force and shouted in triumph as the invasive liquid advanced into the boy's circulatory system at an accelerated rate.

Dirk, stunned by the unexpected turn of events, felt as though his knees were going to give way at any moment; his physical body was failing him. He felt weighted, as if each joint, tendon, and muscle weighed thousands of pounds. Holding himself upright was taking incredible strength that he knew he could not sustain; within seconds he toppled to the ground.

The Senator kicked him over onto his back where he now lay staring up at the jagged rock formations above him. He found he could not cry out because his tongue was too heavy to form syllables. His mouth was closed, and try as he might, he could not part his lips to speak. A dark cloud stood over him, and the Senator's eyes locked on his.

"You are *mine* now! And just to be certain there aren't any unwanted guests around . . ." The Senator's conscious-ness surged into Dirk's mind and began to grow larger and larger.

It simultaneously hurtled forward and backward, explod-ing into different areas of Dirk's mind without warning. It was happening so quickly, and Dirk was so distressed over the physical attack, that he could not begin to think about fighting the Senator off.

"He's sweeping my mind!" Dirk thought. It was only a matter of time until the Senator discovered the psychic link Dirk had forged with Keiko Tan. Dirk tried to bring his men-tal powers under control, to muster the strength to hide the link, but he was not fast enough.

"Aaaaahhhh, what's this? A little connection with Miss Tan, have we? Well, just *imagine* what a surprise she's about to get! This time when the psychic hotline rings, she's going to find an unexpected caller, Mr. Tyrone. Worse yet, I'm afraid I'll be rendering service inoperative. It's time to *sever* this connection permanently."

A thin smile pursed the Senator's lips as he cut the men-tal tie between Dirk and Keiko with unnecessary force. Now that Dirk was helpless and the others were incapable of coming to his assistance, the Senator was drunk with power. Though he had told himself this plan was motivated by the necessity of stabilizing the Merger, his thoughts now turned more to the level of power he would soon wield. He would drain Dirk completely, removing every drop of telepathic energy from the boy, and in the process he would become more powerful than he had ever imagined. He considered whether there would be any limit to what he could accomplish once he had siphoned Dirk's abilities and decided that testing those limits would be a challenge worthy of him. The more he allowed his mind to dwell on these thoughts, the faster his blood seemed to pump.

He dropped to his knees, cupped one hand under Dirk's head, and raised it. Sweat oozed from the boy's scalp and ran through the Senator's fingers, mixing with the dirt that had found its way into Dirk's hair. A rat moved out of a darkened corner, met Dirk's eyes, and froze in its place. The Senator turned to look at the rodent and then brought his face back to Dirk. "He's thinking the table looks set for Thanksgiving dinner, Mr. Tyrone. And he's right! You see, he and his friends are going to pick your bones clean. What a fine meal they shall have! Of course, you needn't worry. By the time I've finished with you, there'll be nothing left of your mind. You won't even realize that they're tearing your flesh apart." The Senator released Dirk's head, and it thudded against the ground painfully. He leaned over Dirk and said icily, "I do hope that's a *comfort,* Mr. Tyrone."

Dirk's eyes blazed. He strained to move his jaw muscles, to open his mouth to speak, but it was no use. Though he could communicate mentally with his attacker, some small part of his inner consciousness told him to remain quiet. The Senator now seated himself behind Dirk's head. "It's time," he said, "to take you apart piece by piece." He grabbed the sides of Dirk's head with his hands, pressing his thumbs into the boy's cheekbones with such intensity that Dirk felt they would surely shatter.

Dirk steeled himself, for he was certain the Senator meant to level his most forceful blows right from the start. That way, he could take what he wanted without much resistance. Surprisingly, that was not how it happened. Instead of lashing out at Dirk's mind with great power and speed, the Senator's mental presence crumbled quickly into very small pieces. Dirk "watched" through his mind's eye as the pieces came to life. They were like fire ants, the Senator told him, that would spread to every nook and cranny of his mind—a deadly chorus led by a sinister conductor. They would sting Dirk in unison and then literally pull his mind apart. His knowledge, his skills, his memories, his . . . *power* . . . would be carted away, like the spoils of war, through a long, dark tunnel that would lead directly into the Senator's mind. It was, in a sense, a massacre of millions with a casualty of one. And it had begun.

Arriving on the scene and finding no sign of Madam or Nicci, Mateo knew instantly that something was very wrong. Seeing no physical sign of danger, he and Mrs. Morph returned to human form while Dr. Pan explained what had happened. Keiko, pale and trembling, described what had happened inside of her mind. "Dirk is in terrible danger." She looked imploringly to Mrs. Morph and Dr. Pan.

"Mrs. Morph," Dr. Pan began, "we must . . ." But before he could finish his statement, she had assumed the shape of a falcon and sped out of sight.

"Hold on there!" Mateo said.

The doctor rested a hand on Mateo's shoulder just as the boy was about to alter form and follow his mentor. "No, Mateo. It is best that you wait with us. It will not take long for her to bring us some information." Within minutes, Nicci Golden appeared before them. It had taken even less time than the doctor expected for Mrs. Morph to produce results.

Nicci was so distraught that she didn't stand before them long enough to speak more than a few words. She simply whisked Dr. Pan to where Madam lay, charging her friends to follow on foot and giving them scant directions just before she and her passenger disappeared. In short order, Mateo, in the guise of a bloodhound, arrived with Keiko at his heels.

Mrs. Morph, who had remained with Madam while Nicci summoned the others, paced to and fro and cracked her gum loudly. "Poor Margie, I never thought he could take her down. She's a fighter—kinda like yours truly!"

Both Mateo and Keiko raised their eyebrows involuntarily.

"Hey listen, kiddos. Margie and me got more in common than just our innate sense of style. Neither one of us is the kinda girl ya wanta mess with 'cause when we really get worked up, things get ugly. Now, I remember this one time when Margie's kid brother J.J. ran a pair of her lavender undies up the flagpole at school. Wow! You shoulda . . ."

"Mrs. Morph!" Dr. Pan stepped away from Madam's form and spoke with a mixture of relief and astonishment. "She has not been harmed. She is sleeping."

"WHAT? Sleeping! Margie's not the kinda gal to sleep on the job, Doc! There's gotta be more to it than that."

"Mrs. Morph, please!" Dr. Pan's tone became rather forceful. "She has been *put* to sleep. I cannot draw the sleep out of her because the suggestion was made mentally, and she is not in pain. But Marcus has Dirk, and we must take action quickly. There is no telling what may be happening even as we speak."

Mateo could not contain his pent-up energy. "We have to go to him! *Now!* Nicci can take us. She could probably take us all if she tried."

Nicci's eyes grew wide. She could *not* take them all. The very thought seemed to steal the oxygen from her lungs. "I can't take five people. I . . . I'm willing to try two but not five. You guys, we'd never make it."

"Matty-boy, we can't leave Margie right now. The three of us have ta stay together until she's come outta this trance. If the Doc and I leave Margie, Marcus could come back and finish her off, and if we take her to him like this, we're just as powerless."

"I'm afraid my colleague is right." Dr. Pan regarded Mateo

and his friends. "It is not an ideal situation, but if Dirk is to have any hope of survival, you three will need to go to him in force."

"Are you *crazy,* Doc? The kiddos can't take Marcus on without help. They aren't ready for that."

"We have to, Teach!" Mateo spoke to her with gentle respect. "You said it yourself. You can't leave Madam alone right now. We have to try. You guys would if the situation were reversed."

"Quickly, Nicci, we must hurry," said Keiko. She feared that every moment of hesitation could be costing Dirk his life.

Dr. Pan's kindly eyes looked to his protégé. "Be safe, child. And return." Keiko nodded in response but said nothing. A tangle of emotions was warring inside of her: concern for her friends, fear of the Senator, and something quite different for Dirk. She had never before been sure how deep her feelings for him ran, but the moment she felt the Senator tearing them apart she had gained the certainty that had eluded her for so long. It was love. What she felt for Dirk was love.

"All right, Matty, let's do this," Nicci said. She looked to Madam's motionless form and wished with all of her being that the woman would awaken. Just a look from Madam, Nicci knew, would help her feel more confident.

"Hey, kid!" Mrs. Morph called to Mateo as he stepped closer to his friends. "Take care of yourself. Ya know what I mean?" Mateo thought he saw her eyes begin to mist.

"See you *soon*, Teach," he replied with a grin, and he and his friends disappeared.

Nicci felt the strain immediately of having two additional people with her as she shifted backward to a time just prior to the Senator's destruction of Keiko and Dirk's link. This allowed Keiko to use the link as a kind of homing beacon—leading Nicci to the entrance of the cave that hid the Senator and his captive from view. The three teens materialized in silence. They heard a grunt from Dirk, which they took to be the Senator's initial attack.

"Let's move ladies," Mateo said. "We don't have much time."

"Wait a minute! We can't just go charging in there without a plan." Nicci found Mateo's impulsivity trying her patience as usual.

"Well what do *you* propose we do, Nicci, ask him if he'd mind not killing our friend?" Mateo's cheeks flushed.

"There is no cause for sarcasm, Matty." Keiko's voice was stern. "We will need to catch the Senator off guard. Then, I suggest we attempt to join with Dirk—allowing him to bring our minds together, much as Madam described the Senator doing for all of them when they were our age."

"That's right. She said it made them all stronger! Let's do it!"

"Matty! Slow it down," Nicci advised. "We have to do things right. If this mind merge doesn't work the way Madam says it does, we're going to be in a whole lot of trouble. I can't get three of you out of here without Dirk's help— especially not in the process of battling with the Senator. Keiko, you've got to make sure Dirk's well enough to do this little psychic trick, and then you've got to tell him that *time* is of the essence."

Keiko nodded agreement, and Mateo slapped his hands together. "Okay, agreed! Nicci, I'll provide the initial distraction—you know—try to throw him off balance. Can you displace him in time? Force him out of the present?"

"I think so. Madam and I were working on something like that before he put her to sleep. In fact, maybe I can shift him in and out of the present rapidly while you attack him physically each time he reappears!"

"And I'll get Dirk ready to bring us all together," Keiko said eagerly. It seemed that their plan had a chance. She hoped so, for all their sakes.

A great grizzly bear rose between the girls and bounded

into the interior of the cave, picking up speed as it moved closer to the Senator, who was literally attempting to consume Dirk's mind. The bear collided with the unwary Senator, knocking the man into the cave wall with great force. "Hey, buddy! You want a piece of me? Huh?" The dazed Senator heard Mateo's voice, and anger boiled the blood inside of him. Somehow, the girl must have found a way to bring them here. He had seriously underestimated her abilities. Very well, he would finish them all at once. But before the Senator could decide where to begin his attack, he found himself flying through time. Suddenly, he was alone on a frozen tundra. He saw what looked like an arctic fox moving stealthily across the mostly barren landscape. "Why you little . . ." The Senator prepared to return himself to the present, but Nicci was one step ahead of him. He was back in the cave in an instant facing the largest marsupial he had ever seen. "Heya, Senator, I'm jumpin' for joy now that you're back again!" Mateo, in the form of an enormous kangaroo, jumped once and then forced his powerful hind legs into the Senator's abdomen, sending the man crashing to the floor.

Whoosh! Senator Broogue was gone from the cave again. He appeared, this time, in a Roman chariot alongside a startled driver who was racing a stallion at breakneck speed. The chariot won the race just as the Senator got his bearings, and cheers erupted from all around. The congratulatory crowd surged forward to envelop the driver, pulling the Senator into the fray as well.

Whoosh! He was back in the cave lying on his back. The Senator started to rise when Mateo, in the guise of a spider, scurried onto his chest. The spider grew to the size of a fairly large horse within seconds. It was a tarantula—weighing the Senator down and moving its fangs toward the man's face.

"Aaaaahhhhhhh!" The Senator cried out in alarm. Though he knew it was Mateo, the creature atop him was horrific, and the sight and weight of it sent adrenaline careening through the Senator's body. He was panicking. Being propelled back and forth through time and trying to maintain a conscious presence in Dirk's mind was keeping him from dealing with the teens effectively.

As Nicci and Mateo continued their onslaught, Keiko made her way to Dirk. The sight of her filled him with hope. *"I'm so sorry!"* His words moved into her mind. *"I shouldn't have come here ... but he told me they were keeping things from us. He told me he could help me learn to strengthen my abilities. He said you were going to be in danger, and I couldn't let that ..."*

"Sshhhh! There will be time later for this." At the touch of her hands, the weighted sensation that had filled Dirk's body moved rapidly into hers. Her body rocked backward, nearly toppling, as her own limbs suffered now from being weighted down. But Keiko's body was healing itself almost as quickly as the weight tried to drag her down, and—in the end—she was victorious.

Dirk jumped to his feet and forced the Senator out of his mind with surprising ease. The man was too distracted to fight Dirk, now fully restored, and deal with Nicci and Mateo. Keiko grabbed Dirk's hands, drawing his attention away from a colossal chicken that was now pecking at the Senator's face.

"Dirk, you must join us—all of us—the way Madam described the Senator doing for them so long ago. We need to be strengthened in order to escape from here. Nicci cannot transport us all without more strength. You need to *merge* our minds. And it's got to work. We will likely have only one chance before the Senator realizes what we are doing. If he stops us ..." She didn't finish. She didn't have to. Dirk knew she was right. They had one shot at escaping, and everything was riding on him.

"C'mon." He pulled her to her feet. The Senator was not

presently in sight, so Dirk called out, "Nicci, Mateo! The next time he appears knock him upside the head and send him to another continent or something. Then, come form a circle with us. We're gonna try creating a little *merger* of our own."

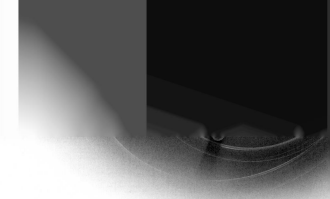

At the Senator's next appearance, he found the very breath squeezed from his lungs by some type of many-tentacled creature Mateo had become. "Enough of this!" the Senator cried out and grimaced in the arms of the creature that held him. He then drew forth every last ounce of his power—preparing to strike Mateo dead with a single blow, but Nicci sent him far off into the galaxy before he was able to attack. Then she grabbed Mateo's hand, and they rushed to Dirk and Keiko.

"Hurry, Matty! He'll bring himself back any minute."

The four of them huddled together, and three pairs of eyes locked on Dirk. He told himself they were looking at him because he was the one who was going to make this happen—the merging of their minds—but somehow he knew that they would have looked to him no matter what the situation had been. He spoke with certainty. There was no reason to let them know how unsure he was. "I want everyone to focus on positive stuff about each other—fill your minds with it!" Dirk's mind became a speedy needle threading its way in and out of the consciousness of each of his friends, stitching them together. He was heartened to find that Matty considered him courageous, and that Nicci admired him when he assumed leadership. The process he was facilitating was like delivering and opening presents, and he could not help but wonder how much more enjoyable it would be if there were more time.

"*Love.*" It was there in Keiko's mind, and the strength of it was so unexpected that it nearly halted his progress. It was love for him, and this was *not* "I love you like a brother"

kind of love. He was stunned; he didn't know how to
respond. He wanted to send something back, but there was-
n't time to get it all formed the right way in his mind—so
that he would sound *cool* yet sincere. He settled for "Yeah,
me too," as he drew the final threads together. They could all
feel Nicci holding the moment, lengthening it, stretching the
time that they were connected in a way that could not be
explained in words. When at last Dirk released the thread
and they separated, it was with a newfound confidence in
themselves and each other. It was, Keiko thought, just as it
had been described to them.

Dirk instantly felt the Senator's mind nearing them. He
was projecting it ahead of his physical body, which would
reappear momentarily.

"He's coming!"

And with no further word, Nicci swept them away in the
blink of an eye.

Senator Broogue found himself standing in an empty cave,
and for a moment he was relieved. He was unaccustomed to
being challenged, let alone beaten. He had a disturbing
sense, too, that Dirk had joined their minds for a time, and
he knew the danger this posed to his plan. He did not howl
with anger, though, nor did he cry out in frustration. He traveled back to the Great Hall. He sat alone and in silence—letting quiet rage feast upon him all through the night.

He would meet Dirk and his friends again soon, in the
past. He still had the advantage, for he knew where Madam
and her friends were going to send them and what they
would be asked to do. Dirk and the others were going to
meet Michael Quinn, the lynchpin in the creation of the
Merger. They were going to meet Michael Quinn, and they
were going to like Michael Quinn very, very much. And then,
in order to achieve the objective that Madam would set
forth, Dirk and his friends were going to have to watch
Michael Quinn die. All four of them would have to battle

against the Senator, who would be trying to save Michael's life, and if just *one* of them weakened, Senator Broogue would strike a deadly blow. He would be victorious, shattering one life and crippling the other three. He would save Dirk for last. The possibility that he might still be able to transplant the boy's power into his own mind had not been discarded. Following the death of his friends, he would be in no position to resist. The Senator could envision it all. He would bring the boy to his knees and then take what he wanted with such force that Dirk wouldn't stand a chance.

Senator Broogue pursed his thin lips into a malevolent grin as he thought of Keiko Tan, the little baby who had distracted him in the hospital so many years ago. She had reminded him of a friendship long dead and caused him to *feel* again. *She* was the key—the weak link among them. She was an empath, a healer; she could never let Michael Quinn die. He knew that she would weaken, and when she did, it would all be over for her . . . and for her friends as well. He wished there were some way for her to know, when the time came, that her weakness would be responsible for the destruction of her friends. "Revenge can be quite a tasty dish to prepare," the Senator mused aloud, *"especially* when you take the time to serve it yourself."

The appearance of the four teens outside the entrance of the Elders' cave startled only a ground squirrel, who went scurrying underground near a fallen limb. They rushed inside—following a series of tunnels that took them far underground to the large meeting space where they had first heard so much of the Elders' story. Madam was still fast asleep, and Dr. Pan, clearly worried, was wringing his hands nervously. As the teens stepped into view, Mrs. Morph ran to Mateo and drew him into a hug that put considerable stress on his rib cage. "I told ya they'd make it!" she cried in triumph. She raced around to each of the teens and engulfed them in her joy.

Dr. Pan's face beamed. Happiness seemed to emanate from inside of him and brighten the entire underground dwelling. "Child," he said looking fondly to Keiko. "I . . ." She kissed his cheek gently and took his hand. "You were with me, Doctor," she pointed to her heart, "in here." Dr. Pan adjusted the head strap that held his little mirror and looked down as his face turned several shades of red.

Mrs. Morph had just released Dirk, the last of her welcome home victims, when she announced what was obvious, "Margie's still not back with us." She looked to Dirk. "Okay, kid, you gotta do some a that jazzy-in-the-head stuff you do and wake her up. The strain of leadership is takin' a toll on this girl right here. If ya know what I mean."

"Can do," Dirk replied. He saw no need to mention that he had been partially responsible for sedating Madam. Either the others knew and did not care, or they did not know at all, in which case telling them right now did not seem like the best idea. He would, though, need to confess what he had done to Madam herself. Dirk directed a strong thought of awakening into her mind. He wanted her to leave sleep and awaken fully restored, alert, and prepared. And she did—so much so that at first she mistakenly thought she was still working with Nicci in the training area.

It quickly became apparent to Madam that she was out of step with recent goings-on, and a full review of the day's events began. Mrs. Morph occasionally interjected comments as she portioned out a very spicy concoction of rice and meat onto plates that were passed around the circle. "Now, had ita been *me* in there with Marcus, Matty-boy, I woulda just become somethin' real big and ugly and bit his head off and spit it out in the corner. And right after I did that, I woulda . . ."

Madam's eyes began to bulge. "Mrs. Morph! That will do. *Really!*"

Mrs. Morph elbowed Mateo and grinned at everyone. "Gets her every time! I love it."

The group suppressed their giggles a bit until Madam glanced up from her plate and quite unexpectedly began to chortle. "Well, one must admit, a headless Senator Broogue would be a bit humorous!"

And now the entire room, if it could be called that, filled with random stories and descriptions of how it could have happened, what would have happened next, and such. Mrs. Morph took over numerous times to tell, with great exaggeration they all knew, how it would have been if *she* had really gotten fired up.

As the hour grew late, Dirk hoped Madam would finally share with them all of the details she was still holding back. But she appeared ready to say nothing more as she bid them all a good rest. "Marcus will stay far from us this night. You may rest well." As she made ready to leave the common area, it was all Dirk could do to keep from entering her mind and directing her to tell them more. He decided instead to follow her and was surprised when she did not move toward the hallway leading to her chambers. Instead, she followed the series of tunnels that led toward the entrance of the cave, and Dirk followed cautiously, a few paces behind. He peered over a boulder just to the left of the entrance, but she seemed to have vanished.

"HUH!" He jerked around, startled as someone tapped his shoulder.

"Maybe you should just *ask* me where I'm going." It was Madam Moment herself. She had shifted back in time and come up behind him. "You are *not* a very good spy, Mr. Tyrone." There was no trace of malice in her voice, for which Dirk was thankful. "Come," she said, indicating that he should move outside of the shelter to the clearing, "let's talk for awhile."

Dirk settled himself on the ground and clasped his hands together in front of him. He began shifting his feet nervously. It was guilt that was keeping him a silent prisoner, and he knew it.

"Mr. Tyrone?" Madam was going to make him go first.

"Look, I . . . uh . . . I've got to be honest with you. I . . . I . . . well, I sort of helped Senator Broogue put you to sleep." His mouth was a desert that would never feel moisture again.

Silence. She was looking up toward the moon. Dirk regarded her white robe. The material seemed to him to be always shiny and new. She was a resplendent and powerful figure—a gifted leader. How had he ever dared to betray her? *Betrayal.* It was the word he had been avoiding, but it was the truth. He *was* a traitor, not only to Madam but to all of them! He could only guess what Senator Broogue might have done if he had been successful in adding Dirk's power to his own. Whatever the man had been planning, it could not have been anything good; Dirk was now certain of that. Silence. He wished she would say something. Anything. Silence, he realized, could be a punishment all its own.

"You *chose* to do this?" she posed the question in a tone that could not be read.

"Yes, Ma'am." What was he doing calling her *Ma'am?* He was so jumbled up inside! Suddenly, he could not contain himself another minute. He began to tell her the whole truth—about how the Senator had played on his suspicions, and how he, Dirk, had insisted that Madam not be harmed, and how he had been afraid for Keiko, and so he had had to take action. Everything spilled out and fell from his lips at her feet, but she did not respond the way he hoped. Even as he poured his truth out to her, he could tell she was not going to absolve him of responsibility. When he stopped and looked up at her, her face was serene but mysterious—a puzzle he could not solve.

"You will find, Dirk, that *trust* is an incredibly difficult gift to truly give someone. It should not come the way that you seem to want it—with conditions." Madam fixed him with her gaze. "I will trust you *if* you tell me what I want to know, *if* you give me what I want, *if* you do as I wish. Conditional trust is not really trust at all. It is an exchange, and as I believe you now know, it can have deadly consequences. There is much that I have kept from you and your friends because, for now, it is best. When the time is right, you will be told. You see, Dirk, *timing* is sometimes critical. Training will continue for the next several days, and it will include practice in the joining of your minds. While I regret that there is no one to mentor you, I believe you can develop your skills on your own to some extent. I will serve as advisor to you as best I can."

"But do you *forgive* me?" Nothing else she had said mattered to Dirk right now. "I'm trying to tell you, I'm sorry. I was wrong. I . . . betrayed you. Betrayed the whole group, but mostly you, and I'm just . . . well, I'm sorry."

Madam moved forward and in a gesture of tenderness he was not accustomed to from her, she took his hands in hers. "I *trust* you, Dirk. *Still.*" An owl called from the woods, the breeze stirred, and she was gone.

CHAPTER 15

O ver the next several days, the Elders worked with their "students" to harness and expand their abilities to a level far beyond what the teens had ever dreamed possible. Breaks, if they could be called that, were spent with Dirk joining their minds to further increase their confidence and sense of support for one another. It was after completing one of these sessions that Mrs. Morph spoke up.

"Hey, Margie, I got me an idea. What say the next time the kiddos merge, we get in on a little of the action. Ya know? Sort of a *double dipper!* Whatdaya say?"

The corners of Madam's lips turned down. "Mrs. Morph, the very idea! It's simply preposterous. We shall not go gallivanting into their minds as if we are on some sort of theme-park ride. They have established a merger of their own. It is quite private and should remain as such."

Unflappable as always, Mrs. Morph simply looked at Dr. Pan and said, "Geez! She coulda just said 'no.'"

Dr. Panacea patted his colleague's hand gently, and much to everyone's surprise, spoke in support of her suggestion. "Madam, I believe her idea is deserving of a much more serious discussion." He started to grab for his stethoscope but stopped himself. Instead, he looked directly at Madam as opposed to down at the ground, as was his tendency when even minor conflict arose.

The teens looked from Dr. Pan to Madam. They had never heard him disagree with her so strongly before, but the look of shock they expected to find on Madam's face was undetectable. She looked kindly at the doctor and acquiesced. "Doctor, please continue. Perhaps we should all be seated."

Dr. Pan, Keiko knew, did not like being in the spotlight. They were much alike in that regard. It was difficult for him, she knew, to challenge Madam's decision. He spoke now with the sense of certainty that Keiko had heard in his voice during her training. "Time is growing short, Madam. They must leave us soon . . ."

A startled gasp from all of the teens but Dirk was audible. "So," he thought, "we're finally going to learn what this is all about." He was not surprised to learn that he and his friends would be leaving; he simply wanted to know where they were going . . . and why.

Sensing the restlessness his statement had caused, Dr. Pan paused. "I have upset them. I am sorry. It is not in my nature to cause others to . . ."

"Doctor, they will survive a few moments of discomfort. Continue." Madam's words were gentle.

"Well, it seems to me that a *collective* merger, assuming Dirk can handle three more of us and that the others are willing, might allow us to leave something a bit more *permanent,* so to speak." The doctor steadily held his colleague's eyes. "It could make the difference, Madam. *All the difference.*"

Mrs. Morph regarded her two colleagues with apprehension. "Ya know there's no goin' back if we do this—this that he's suggestin' we do, Margie." She looked then at Mateo in a fixed gaze that held him motionless for a moment. She turned back to Madam, "But, hey, I'm in—you can count on me! I mean this girl always brings a gift to the party. Wouldn't be right to take it with me when I left—if ya know what I mean."

Madam's admiration for her colleagues emanated from her in such a way that Dirk could not keep from sensing it. It was almost tangible, like something you could pick up and hold and never let go. "Mrs. Morph," Madam spoke with uncharacteristic emotion, "I know *exactly* what you mean."

Dirk and the others could not decipher exactly *what* their mentors were discussing, but it was obviously very serious. It was clear the idea of a joint merger with all seven of their minds was on the table as a discussion item, but what did the doctor mean about leaving something behind permanently?

"Mr. Tyrone," Madam's voice returned to its typical authoritative tone. "You have had ample practice in the process of merging four minds. Would you be willing to try seven? It will be more taxing, but I've no doubt you are up to the task."

"Sure I can do it, but . . ."

"I have not finished, Mr. Tyrone. All of you shall have a say in this. We are asking you to share what has become a very private experience with three outsiders. It would be understandable if any of you felt uncomfortable . . ."

"Outsiders?" Nicci blurted it out with disgust. She had never imagined speaking in such a way to Madam, but she couldn't seem to stop herself. "How can you use that word after what we've shared together? *Why* did you use it?" Finally, her tone became gentle. "Madam, why do you always seem to be at a distance?"

Madam slowly shook her head. "I never intended . . ."

A heaviness was hanging in the air—like too much dirty laundry. Mateo decided to do something about it and cut right into Madam's sentence with a question. "What's with the names?"

Mrs. Morph, seated next to him as usual, grabbed his elbow and spoke a bit too loudly into his ear, "Matty, I told ya before about this problem with interruptin'. We *both* gotta work on it! Now let Margie . . ."

"No, Teach. I want to know." He looked directly at Madam. "Why the superhero names? Madam *Moment,* Mrs. *Morph,* Dr. *Panacea!* I mean, come on! I've been wondering from the beginning, but now I just gotta know. What's with the dorky names?"

Though they all had wondered and talked about it among themselves, no one had dared to ask. Nicci was angry that Mateo hadn't allowed Madam to explain herself! His timing was off, as usual, as far as she was concerned. "Mateo, this isn't the time . . ."

"Correction, Miss Golden, it is a fine time." Madam's composure was back in place. "Mr. Rodriguez, the *dorky* names, as you put it, were a decision we made to protect you. You see, we felt that titles of some sort would distance us from you. First names lend themselves to more intimate relationships, and we needed to be your protectors, not your friends. I felt this was immensely important."

"We feared that if we became too fond of you," Dr. Pan continued, "we might not be able to think objectively and thus we could place you in danger. Sometimes it is easier to see and to do what is best for people when you are not emotionally involved with them."

"Actually," Madam took over again, "we had agreed to speak to each of you more formally; however, it appeared quite early on that *I* was the only one who would hold to that end of the bargain."

Nicci realized that Madam was right. It was usually "Miss Golden or Mr. Tyrone," with her.

"I . . . uh . . . I got to do the names." Mrs. Morph looked at Mateo, "Do ya really think they're dorky? Ya know I was thinkin' about *Chameleon Girl* for me. Maybe I shoulda gone with that one, huh, Matty?"

Everyone groaned aloud, including Madam Moment.

Keiko reached over and touched the doctor's hand. "No disrespect intended, Madam, but your plan to create emotional distance has not worked."

"Indeed," Madam replied with a warm smile.

"Well, I know I interrupted and all, but I just . . . things were getting too intense, okay?" Mateo stumbled through what he meant to be an apology as quickly as he could.

"Your goal was admirable, Mr. Rodri . . . Mateo. Thank you. Now, if there are no further objections, it will be agreed that the seven of us will in fact, merge when the *time* is right. That time is not now, but it shall come all too soon." Madam adjusted her robe as her voice changed in timbre to that of a storyteller. "It is time, my friends, to tell you the story of a young man named Michael Quinn. It is a story you will come to know intimately because, very soon, you will all meet Michael. And, I fear, you may come to care about him very much."

"This guy was born to shake things up in the world—a little like yours truly if ya don't mind my sayin' so. I mean he had charisma and big ideas. He was the kinda guy who could motivate people to care about things they never cared about before." Mrs. Morph spoke of Michael Quinn as though she was well acquainted with him, or at least with his story.

"Michael was shot one evening—trying to save the life of an elderly woman during a robbery; she survived, but he lost his own life in the process. It was a tragedy. A senseless loss of life." Dr. Pan's voice was heavy with sadness.

"This, you must understand, was in *real* time—the true timeline of our world. The past as it was *intended* to be." Madam had taken up the story again. "Every now and again, a person comes into this world who stands to make tremendous contributions. Such people bring about significant changes themselves or in some cases, like that of Michael Quinn, set in motion a chain of events that result in altering the thinking and decisions of entire societies. After years of traveling into the past and exploring the alternate timelines of various individuals, Marcus stumbled upon Michael and discovered a way to bring about his dream of a merged culture, one in which there would no longer be a multiracial element. All he had to do . . . was *save* Michael Quinn's life."

The doctor's eyes were intense as he picked up the narration. "Marcus learned that if Michael had not died that

night, he would have gone on to college. While he was con-
sumed with his studies there, a war would break out overseas. A war waged over racial issues. This country's
involvement would be delayed due to a tremendous outcry
from citizens—fueled by protests that sprang from college
and university campuses all over the country. Michael
Quinn led the first protest riots on his own campus, and
they were highly successful. Before he knew it, he was
speaking all over the country, inciting his peers to protest as
well. The fervor and passion spread from the university
campuses to people of all ages, and the pressure on the government to delay entry into the war became monumental.
The two-year delay brought on by the protests cost hundreds of thousands of lives overseas."

"Finally, upon our entry into the war, a quick and decisive
end was reached." Madam's voice was filled with regret as
she played out the sequence of events that followed the
war's end. "Marcus directed situations and manipulated
leaders in such a way that, over time, the Legion for World
Alliance was formed; it was and is today a governing body
for the entire world—and the idea for the Merger came
along with it. After such a bloody war—fought primarily
over racial issues—the world was ripe for Marcus' ideas. He
adopted the title of Senator Broogue and assumed the
appearance you recognize today—one that hides his
Caucasian features. His mental abilities brought him all of
the power and influence necessary from that point on to create the Merger.

"The world's finest scientists came together under
Marcus' direction, and together they developed a serum that
altered DNA so that certain physical characteristics of
humans such as skin tone, shape and color of the eye, and
hair color would be the same for everyone. When the serum
was perfected, it was administered to people worldwide in
the form of a vaccine that was promised to protect them

from a new and deadly virus." She paused for a moment and noted that Dirk and his friends appeared to be listening carefully. "Of course, there *was* no deadly virus; the two real purposes of the vaccine were kept secret. First, it served to alter the DNA of any conceived human embryo in such a way that the physical characteristics of the baby would represent a merging of races—just as you know it to be today."

"But what about all the people already walking around the planet!" Mateo's curiosity forced him to interrupt the story. "They were just like us; they weren't merged. Wouldn't they wonder why all of their babies started looking freaky?"

Madam cocked an eyebrow at the interruption. "You will recall, Mr. Rodriguez, that I stated the vaccine had *two* purposes?" He nodded quickly while looking at the ground in embarrassment, and Madam continued. "The serum used for the vaccine contained elements of Marcus' blood that rendered people extremely vulnerable to a suggestion he gave to entire countries en masse. He planted the image of a merged society in people's minds—the idea that they had always looked this way, that *everyone* had always looked this way, became natural."

"So when people looked in the mirror, they didn't see *themselves* anymore?" Keiko directed her question to the doctor.

He shook his head sadly. "They saw what Marcus wanted them to see," he said. "And, once the suggestion was implanted in their minds, it remained with them. Even pictures in books or movies—anything that might suggest evidence of racial diversity—were viewed by the people through Marcus' eyes for a while. He couldn't keep up that level of control for long, so the Alliance began taking extraordinary action. Pulling books and burning them, banning any printed or electronic document that made mention of, or pictured people with, any sense of racial identity. Over the course of several years, necessary documentation was remade or falsified until, finally, there was nothing left to suggest that a time before the Merger existed."

Nicci drew in a breath at the enormity of it all. "An entire generation of people went to their graves with the truth of who they were, racially anyway, literally stolen from them," she said.

Madam nodded. "And the children born of that generation and each generation that followed never knew the difference. The Merger was complete."

"Marcus was mindful, though," Dr. Pan pointed out, "that the mutated genes in *our* bodies might manifest themselves at some point down the line. And this he had great cause to fear."

"He said he was my ancestor," Dirk said with contempt, "and you guys are saying it's true?"

Madam responded, "It *is* true, Mr. Tyrone, and the suggestion provided a very compelling reason for you to seek him out, did it not? We *are* your ancestors from quite some time ago—exactly how long is unimportant. Our abilities have allowed us tremendous longevity of life, and that has been necessary so that we could be here for you now. You and your friends—your existence—is the only threat to the world Marcus has fashioned."

Dirk finally understood. "So *that's* why he's been so desperate to get rid of us. That's why Aunt Lisa hid us for so many years! She wasn't just hiding us from the Alliance because we were *different*. She was hiding us from *him*."

"She always told us it would be terribly dangerous for anyone to see us," Nicci said, "but she wouldn't say why. She should have at least told us about the Senator."

"Sweetie," Mrs. Morph pinched her cheek. "You didn't wanta know all this when you was a tyke. Take it from a girl who knows—the lady did what was best for ya."

Keiko had been listening so intently that when she began to speak, she nearly startled herself. "But how did you learn all of this, Madam?"

"I have traveled into the past and seen what he has done. I have witnessed him involving himself in history so that the timeline was altered, but I could not stop him. He is far too powerful for me to defeat alone. Furthermore, some type of mental markers are in place so that it is not possible for any of us to become involved in Michael Quinn's life without Marcus knowing."

"You want *us* to go back and stop him. That's it!" Dirk stood and paced the room. It was finally all coming together for him. "Nicci's supposed to take us all back in time. We're supposed to meet this Michael Quinn guy and . . ."

"And *we* will have to make certain that he gets shot." Mateo uttered the words no one else wanted to say.

Keiko's head was shaking "no" involuntarily. How could she ever be party to allowing someone's death? No matter what the reason, it simply was not possible. Surely they knew she could not do it. *Would not* do it. "I can't." She said the words and offered no further explanation.

"Child," Dr. Pan touched her shoulder gently. "There is only one way to destroy the Merger. Michael Quinn must die."

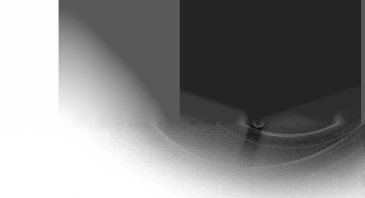

A fitful night for Keiko led to restlessness for Dirk as well. Over the course of the last few weeks their psychic link had been restored, and their relationship had blossomed. Parts of her dreams frequently made their way into his mind—and when he was the main character, it was particularly nice.

Tonight, though, was quite different. Tonight Michael Quinn had been shot over and over again . . . and each time, while the others had fought to keep the Senator from changing Michael's fate, Keiko had betrayed them. She had fallen on wet pavement on a side street of a city where only the glow of the moon cast light by which she could see, and she had saved Michael Quinn's life repeatedly. The dream sequence was running again, nearing the end, but this time something was different. As the robber ran away, Keiko knelt beside the fallen boy and placed her hands on him to draw away his pain. Instantaneously, Michael's eyes became devilish! He grabbed her wrists harshly and laughed as he morphed into the shape of Senator Broogue.

Her high-pitched scream erupted through the cave tunnels and reverberated all around. Dirk bolted from his bed and raced toward the sleeping area Keiko and Nicci occupied, but his mental self moved far ahead of him. He burst into her mind with practiced ease, ready to do battle against the Senator, but he was not there. He had not been there; it had only been a dream.

Despite his best effort, Dirk was the last one to physically show up in Keiko's room. By the time he got there, Dr. Pan was sitting next to her offering comfort while Madam looked on. Dirk was interested in being the one to comfort Keiko, but not in front of everyone else. He hoped they'd all head back to bed soon. If so, he could stick around, convince Nicci to go for a walk, and spend some time alone with Keiko.

"Uh, Dirk," Mateo's voice registered concern in a good-natured sense. "Buddy, I . . . uhhh . . . I think you forgot something."

"Huh?" Dirk's eyes were fixed on Keiko and the doctor.

Madam's bemused voice spoke softly, "Mr. Tyrone—it appears you forgot to *dress* yourself before careening in here to save the fair maiden."

"What? Huh! Oh . . . heh! Heh! Yeah! Uh . . ." Dirk could feel his cheeks flushing. He stared down at his boxer shorts in wonder.

Mrs. Morph walked over and slapped him on the rear. "Aaaahh! It's okay, kid. A young stallion like you oughta run around half-naked every now and then. It's good for the . . ."

"MRS. MORPH!" Madam was aghast.

"Digestion! Yeah, that's what I was going to say, kid. It's good for the digestion." One look at Mrs. Morph told everyone that she was actually going to say something quite different. "Now get outta here and back to bed. Everybody! I get a little cross when I don't get my beauty sleep. Not that this girl needs a lota that! And *you*," she grabbed Mateo and pulled him off to the side as the others headed out. "Don't you go gettin' no ideas about runnin' into anyone's room without bein' sure you're dressed, Matty-boy!"

"But you just said . . ."

"I *know* what I said. But that was someone else's kid. When it comes to mine . . ." She stopped suddenly—awkwardly aware of what she had just said. What was she saying—*mine?* He wasn't *hers.* He was a *student*—someone she was training in a skill, nothing more. So why did she feel this way? Why did she constantly want to fix his hair and warn him of every danger she could anticipate? Why did she not want him to date until he was thirty-two? "Listen, Matty. It's late. I get a little crazy in the head when it's late, ya know. I don't know what I'm tryin' to say."

He leaned over and kissed her on the cheek. "I do, Teach. G'night." He morphed into a tabby cat and bounded away.

Mrs. Morph looked wistful and touched the place on her cheek where Mateo had kissed her. She wondered at the tremendous growth of her concern for him and his friends over the past weeks as she glanced off in the direction the tabby had run. "G'night, Matty. Sweet dreams."

Dirk and his friends could feel the Elders becoming more anxious as their training intensified over the next few days. The late afternoon sessions where the teens merged became a welcome relief from the rigors of their instruction. On this particular day, they were met with a surprise when they arrived at the place where they typically joined minds—the Elders were waiting for them.

"If you are still in agreement with regard to allowing us to share in a merging of minds with you," Madam stated solemnly, "we would like this to be the day. We have taught you as much as we can. The *time* is right, both for your journey into the past and for us to say our goodbyes."

"What?" Nicci couldn't help but speak first. She had spent more time with Madam than the others. "Just like that? What about some advance notice? I mean, don't we get a little time to prepare? Ask a few questions? I mean, how do you expect us to just . . ."

Madam walked over and squared Nicci's shoulders. "Nichelle," she began and then paused for a moment. Nicci smiled, despite herself. Though she didn't usually like being called by her given name, Madam's voice made it sound lovely. "Your words come quickly when you become nervous," Madam continued. "You must remember to maintain your focus—even when your emotions would lead you astray."

"Maybe so. But I can't believe what I'm hearing. We're going to merge right now—in just a few minutes, and then it's time to go? You know, you really should think about . . ." Nicci's voice was cracking as she spoke, and then, suddenly, the tears she had been holding back spilled forward. Madam pulled the girl into an embrace that was clearly welcomed, and though no words were exchanged, the elder woman laid aside talk of the plan for a few moments.

"It is what makes her a good leader. It is, in fact, what makes *all* exceptional leaders," Dr. Pan spoke quietly to Dirk who was carefully watching the scene before them. "Knowing when someone doesn't need you to lead but instead to give of yourself in a different way."

Madam stepped away from Nicci and regained her composure. "I'd like us to be seated." She became quite businesslike again and began a circle with Dirk and Nicci on either side of her. "Miss Golden, you are well prepared," said Madam, "to take the offensive and use your abilities as a weapon when needed. I am quite confident in this." Nicci nodded as scenes from her training over the past few weeks flashed through her mind. She felt proud that her abilities were more sophisticated than the Senator's when it came to time travel, but she was still worried. Knowing that Madam would not be with her—to coach her or, for that matter, to *save* her—was unsettling.

"Remember, too," Madam continued, "that Marcus can bring a very forceful mental attack against any of you as he follows you through time." She looked to Dirk. "Mr. Tyrone, you will remember your little adventure with a certain giant?" Sweat broke out across Dirk's brow, and he gave an internal shudder at the mention of his childhood nightmare-come-to-life. "I am directing *all of you* to respond to an attack from Marcus by retaliating against him. While he is quite powerful, he is not accustomed to being resisted. I believe the four of you, collectively, will prove most intimidating to him."

Keiko found it hard to believe that the Senator could be intimidated by anyone or anything. "Madam, he has years of experience. Even with the training you have given us, how can we hope to . . ."

Madam cut her off before she could finish, "Miss Tan, *all* members of the human race have weaknesses. Even Marcus."

"Yeah, but . . ." A look from Mrs. Morph silenced Mateo's interruption. He grinned and closed his mouth. She gave him the thumbs up.

Madam began again. "Miss Golden will ensure your safe arrival at some point in time *before* the night that Marcus saves Michael Quinn. While in the past, you will meet Michael and manage, somehow, to be with him on that fateful evening. The Senator will, of course, be there as well. It goes without saying that he will do everything in his power to stop you."

"But can't you just take us right to the scene or to just a few minutes before it?" Dirk asked. The less time spent in the past the better, as far as he was concerned.

"Yeah! Maybe we could get in and out really fast before he can put up a fight!" Mateo felt an adrenaline rush at the thought of defeating the Senator once again.

"The farther back in time you go, the more difficult it is to pinpoint events with the type of precision you are suggesting," Madam responded, "especially when you don't have years of practiced experience. The Senator has mastered the time period surrounding the robbery. He may be expecting you to show up on that very night. A disparity in your anticipated arrival may catch him unaware," Madam responded.

"It's important," Nicci told her friends, "to blend in. We need to restore the natural order of the past, but we *don't* want to alter anything else while we're there."

Dirk noted how much Nicci was starting to sound like her mentor. Her comment about restoring the natural order of time suggested a new and deeper understanding of her abilities and the responsibility they carried.

Keiko feared she knew the answer to the question she had been pondering since this discussion began. She had hoped someone would raise the issue for her, but no one had done so. Time was drawing short, so she would have to be the one. "Madam, even if we *are* successful, what's to keep the Senator from simply returning to the past and altering things again?"

Madam's colleagues regarded her with a look that indicated this had been a discussion they had held before—in private. When she did not speak, Nicci chose to do so.

"We're going to have to stay there and guard against it, aren't we?" She did not look happy at the prospect. How could she possibly hold everyone in the past indefinitely and keep them all from creating any serious disruptions in the timeline?

Madam sighed. "Nicci's analysis is one possibility." An awkward pause followed as the weight of Madam's words began to work against the normal rhythm of Nicci's breathing.

"Another possibility is that Marcus may be wounded in the battle." Dr. Pan's eyes met his listeners head on as he spoke. "Fatally wounded, I mean." He looked to Keiko whose eyes were wide. "Understand I am not asking or even suggesting that you destroy him," Dr. Pan assured her. "I am simply saying that there is a possibility that he will not survive the ordeal."

"But you *are* saying it's either him or us!" Mateo wanted action. Now. No more talking about possibilities. "Well, I say bring it on!"

"There are," Madam's voice became soft, "many possibilities. We have spoken only of two. It is time now for Dirk to join us all as one." She looked then to her colleagues and smiled affectionately. Dirk thought he was the only one to notice the small nods they gave her in return.

"There's something *more* going on here," he thought. "There's something they're not telling us." He had sensed Madam and the others guarding a portion of their thoughts from him for days. He could easily have probed their minds and discovered the secret—but not without their knowledge. "Well, pretty soon there won't be any more secrets," he told himself as the group stood and began to move into a tight circle.

It was time for him to merge the old and the young, the mentors with the apprentices. And it struck him then, the irony of it; the creation of one merger would likely bring about the destruction of another. What Dirk did not realize until it was far too late, was that this merger would bring an end to more than just the altered timeline Senator Broogue had created. For within seconds of joining the minds around him, Dirk was privy to the secret Madam and her friends had so carefully protected. *This* merger would mark the end of the Elders' lives.

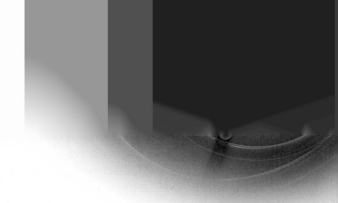

irk instinctively shielded his friends from the knowl-edge of his discovery while tackling the subject with the Elders. All communication was now handled mentally, and Dirk became somewhat of a traffic cop for conversations. He needed to talk to the Elders in private for a few minutes, and that was the only explanation he could give his friends as, mentally, he put them in a room behind a locked door for a few minutes.

"All right! Somebody better start with some answers and fast. You guys are dying? Let's see, did mentioning that just sort of slip your minds? I can't seem to remember your men-tioning it. How is that even possible? Why didn't you tell us? Who's going to tell them? It'll crush them. Keiko! Keiko! Can you even imagine? Doctor, what good is she going to be when she finds this out? You should have prepared us. You should have . . ."

Madam knew Dirk's outrage was motivated by affection. *"Dirk, we are not dying."*

Relief swelled within him. *"Oh! Wheeewww! Well, I'm sure glad to hear that. But how come you're all thinking . . ."*

"Our lives, as you know us, will end shortly," Dr. Panacea continued. *"But by choice."*

"Listen, kid." He thought he could hear the crack of Mrs. Morph's gum even in mental conversation. *"We gotta give you kiddos the best chance at success. Ya hear what I'm sayin' to ya? So, we're dumpin' all our extra juice into you."*

"What? You can't be serious! I don't know how to use your abilities! I . . . I . . . don't want them. I'm doing fine. We all are! We can do this, you guys. You . . . you gotta have faith in

us." Dirk was unprepared for the emotion of the moment; this discussion of finality stirred an unpleasant memory he had carefully buried. Without warning, he heard the desperate cries from his aunt escaping from the safe place he had secured them ever since her death. He could not bear another loss.

"*Dirk . . .*" Madam began.

He did not let her continue. His mental voice released halting words in an attempt to hold his emotions in check. "*They need you—my friends, that is. You know that, don't you? They really need you guys, a lot. I . . . uh . . . I don't think they'll . . .*" His voice cracked, and he knew that his physical body was experiencing a heaving of the chest. "*Please . . .*"

"*Dirk, you will understand one day that we had no other choice. This will give you a tremendous advantage over Marcus—one that he will never anticipate.*" Madam's thoughts were filled with hope. "*You have been alone in many ways these past weeks, Dirk, with no one to truly guide you in the use of your abilities. Now, you will have a part of us with you.*"

Dr. Pan bubbled with excitement. "*We have no way to know how each of our powers will manifest itself in you, Dirk. Trust, though, that it will happen. We are certain that your mental skills will be an aid in helping you decide when and how best to use them.*"

"*But don't go tellin' Matty and the others! Big no-no, there, kid. Marcus would find out.*"

"*Mrs. Morph is right, Dirk. This information must be kept secret. At all costs you must protect this information from Marcus, and that means keeping it from your friends. He would read it in their minds in an instant. Your mind, though, will be much more difficult for him to invade.*" Madam's thinking on the matter was firm, and though Dirk didn't like keeping something so important from his friends, he knew that, as usual, she was right.

Was that what made Madam a good leader—the fact that she was always right? He wondered. Or maybe being right wasn't the important thing, maybe it was being decisive and confident. There was so much he wanted to ask her, selfishly, so that he could know how best to lead his friends. Yes, he *was* going to lead them; he knew that now. Not because *he* needed to do it but because they needed him to do it.

He considered each of the Elders for a moment and realized what a privilege it had been to know them. He understood, too, something about valor and heroism that he had not realized before. It did not come, always, dressed in armor, moving in tanks, riding on horses, or carrying weapons. It was not found, as some might believe, only in men or only in the young. No, it came in every size and every shape, in every gender and every age. And every race. He reminded himself that the Elders knew what they were doing. They knew right from wrong. They knew and understood *truth* far better than he had given them credit for, and they were willing to make the ultimate sacrifice to do what was right. He would not fail them.

"We must say goodbye to your friends now," Dr. Pan's thoughts were sorrowful. *"You will explain to them, when it is safe to do so, what we have done and why?"*

"Yeah, sure," Dirk responded to the doctor while mentally opening the door behind which his friends had been waiting.

"Well it's about time!" Mateo's thoughts bordered on anger. He didn't like it that Dirk and the Elders were speaking alone. *"I was starting . . ."*

Nicci silenced him. *"Matty, let it go. This isn't the time. Just . . . let it go."*

At last, the seven of them came together in a merging of minds unlike anything they ever could have imagined. The confidence, love, and trust shared by all became building blocks they could use to create stamina and a unity of purpose that was needed for the task ahead. When the time came, general goodbyes were shared all around. Then, Dirk created a private place for each mentor and apprentice to spend a few moments together. With his aid, they were even able to experience their mental conversations as though they were taking place *physically*. Dirk felt it was necessary that they be able to speak and to touch, or at least to *think* that's what was happening. He wanted to do all that he could to make these moments memorable for his friends since they did not realize that these were truly final goodbyes.

Nicci did not wait for Madam to move first but immediately embraced the woman with a warm and energetic hug that was returned with surprising fervor. "You have changed my life these past few weeks, Madam," said Nicci. "You've given me the confidence I didn't have. I'm not so afraid anymore. Thank you."

The older woman touched Nicci's check softly, "I have given you only a chance to see all that you can do, my dear. And you have made the most of it. I shall think of you with great fondness, Nichelle. Make the most of the time you are given. Every moment is precious."

"Doctor," Keiko spoke earnestly as she walked, or rather envisioned herself walking, hand in hand with her mentor, "I wish you were my grandfather."

"Heavens, child. I am far too old for that—older, in fact, than you would even guess. My colleague has held back the hands of time for us. But if it helps you to think of me as your grandfather, I should be quite delighted!" He giggled a bit and reached for his stethoscope.

"Well, *Grandfather,* it does help me. So *thank* you." She smiled then. A smile that might heal the pain of an entire planet if such a thing were possible. "Thank you for everything. I will miss you so much over the next . . ." She laughed aloud. "Oh, who knows how long it will really be in *this* time period. Well, however long it is, it will be too long to be away. It will be better when we are back together again."

Dr. Panacea placed his withered hands to each side of Keiko's face and kissed her forehead. "It may seem long, child, but that is why we are given memories. Take care of your friends, Keiko. Guard their lives jealously. To the best of your ability, care for and respect all living creatures. Remember that it is in caring for others that we ultimately care for ourselves."

Within seconds of being alone with his mentor, Mateo tried to launch them into a game of *paper, scissors, rock*—metamorph style. Mrs. Morph had beaten him yesterday by becoming a parasite that attacked his wooly mammoth; Mateo was itching for a rematch. When she did not transform in response to his king cobra, he slithered over and returned to his natural appearance. "Hey, Teach, what gives? Don't I get a chance to take you on again before I hit the road?"

"Well, ya know, Matty . . ." and that's when her voice broke. Tears she had not anticipated, had never in a million years expected, began cascading down her cheeks like swiftly moving streams. She raised her hands to her face.

Mateo was taken completely off guard. "Teach. Hey! Hey, wait a minute." He came over and placed his arm gently around her. "What's with the waterworks?"

"I just got somethin' in my eye, okay? All right? You got a problem with that?" Her voice was full of exaggerated bluster that he knew to ignore.

"Okay, okay!" He withdrew his arm and started to move away. "Whatever you say, Teach."

She grabbed his arm and held him there. "No. Don't go, Matty. It's just I ain't so good on these goodbyes, ya know? I mean, me, I'm the kinda girl who's real soft-spoken. No one ever knows what's goin' on in the ole noggin here," she pointed to her head. "If ya know what I mean."

"Uh, yeah, Teach. I . . . uh . . . know what you mean. I've always thought of you as the soft-spoken type," he said grinning.

"Yeah, okay then. So . . . ya know. It's sorta hard for me to say . . ." Abruptly, she grabbed Mateo's shoulders and turned him to directly face her. "It's sorta like you're my own kid, okay?" Mrs. Morph became quite loud and suddenly began talking so fast Mateo could barely make it all out. "I never felt like this before, ya know? And I need ya to be all right, Matty. I need ya to *always* be all right! Are ya hearin' me say that? 'Cause if anything ever happened to ya . . . I just want ya to know how I feel and all because, well, because . . . well, people don't say it enough—all this gushy stuff! And it's good for the digestion, Matty. You remember that! Ya hear me talkin' to ya?" And the tears ran and ran as she reached up and tenderly touched his cheek for what she knew would be the last time. Mrs. Morph felt the urgency rising in her own voice, and she knew if she said much more, her loss of control would alert Mateo that this was much more than a short-term goodbye. It was a wonder he hadn't figured it out already. "That's it," she said with a sigh. "That's all I got to say."

He kissed her cheek. *"I love you, too, Teach."*

Dirk felt the Elders' abilities, as well as their conscious minds, spilling into him one by one. It was a feeling unlike anything he had ever experienced. It was tremendously exciting, at first, but he was becoming overwhelmed—quickly. He would be able to keep only *some* of their powers and the knowledge of how to use them. He couldn't possibly manage the mental essence and abilities of all of them. It was simply too much for one mind to contain.

Madam's voice spoke urgently in his head, *"You must sift through our powers more rapidly, Dirk, and discard much of what you find. Take what will serve you best and do not feel guilty. There is no time for that. We knew it would be . . ."*

Silence. She was gone.

The best way to honor their memory was to do just as Madam had asked. Dirk's mind became a giant net catching fragments of their powers, which he mentally sorted through—selecting pieces of what he thought he might need. As he drew in some of Mrs. Morph's ability, Dirk sensed a minor stirring in the minds of the Elders—almost as if they were having a last-minute meeting without him. He wanted to investigate, of course, but there was no time. He had to begin barricading the knowledge of his new abilities in such a way as to keep them safely hidden from his friends and, more importantly, from the Senator. If the Senator discovered just how much he and Dirk were now alike, the Elders would have sacrificed themselves for nothing.

"Nicci!" Dirk's tone of authority ringing in Nicci's mind gave her confidence. He sounded like the leader they all needed him to be. *"It's time. The Elders have left the merger, and as I release the rest of you, we need to move into the past immediately."*

"I'm ready, Dirk. I can do this," Nicci responded without hesitation.

Dirk's greatest fear was of what might happen in the next few minutes. As the merger dissolved, and everyone became aware of their physical bodies again, his friends would no doubt catch a glimpse of the now lifeless bodies of the Elders. If that happened, he knew, all hope would be lost. Skillfully, but with much guilt, he projected a false image into the minds of his friends—one of the Elders standing contentedly and beaming with pride at their "students." His deceit was entirely successful; Matty waved enthusiastically to Mrs. Morph, and Keiko blew a kiss to the doctor that Dirk selfishly wished had been meant for him. Nicci winked at the image of Madam, and in the blink of an eye they were gone. Only Dirk knew that when they returned, *if* they returned, there would be no one waiting to greet them.

Senator Broogue was deep in discussion with two senior officials when he felt the disturbance in time. One of the mental markers he had left surrounding the pivotal moment in Michael Quinn's life was sounding a warning. While the timing was inconvenient, he was not unprepared. He dismissed the men with a flimsy excuse and rubbed his hands together. "So. It has begun. Now, my young friends, you're going to learn a lesson about *home court advantage*. A lesson you would have good reason to remember—if any of you had a future."

irk and his friends were on guard as never before during the trip into the past, but there was no sign of the Senator during the journey. Dirk wasn't sure whether that was good or bad. He had anticipated an attack. When none came, he realized that an adversary who does what is expected is not nearly so fearsome as one who strikes when least expected. Reminding himself that he had some surprises of his own for the Senator reassured Dirk some. But not much.

As their feet touched solid ground—somewhere in the past—Mateo gave a whistle of disapproval at the surroundings. "This place is a dump." They had appeared on the balcony of a rundown apartment building. The rusted metal railings appeared loose in some places and were completely unattached to the support columns in others. The lack of care was evident. Mateo noticed the rust from the railings had spilled out onto the cement balconies making starburst-like pools in places where the metal met the concrete. Gray paint, or what was left of it, gave the apartment doors and trim a weathered appearance, and many of them had outer screen doors that were hanging lopsided. The building was clad with aluminum siding, burnt orange in color. It didn't go with the gray paint but complemented the rusted balcony railings quite well.

"Hey, at least the ride was free," Nicci said somewhat apologetically. As they walked the length of the third-floor balcony, she wondered if the building was occupied. It was so quiet. The position of the sun told her it was mid-afternoon so perhaps everyone was at work. She was curious about why this particular place had seemed the right place for them to enter the past. It did not appear to be the kind of place where they would run into someone who was destined to change the world. "Or fail to change it," she reminded herself. For that is exactly what *would* happen if they were successful. Michael Quinn's life would follow its intended timeline; he would not change the world because he would not live to do so. Nicci wished they knew more details about the night of his death.

The rumble of a large engine, followed by an unmistakable shade of yellow, drew everyone's attention away from the run-down appearance of the apartment building. A school bus stopped just a few yards from the building, and children spilled forth and covered the ground like ants at an abandoned picnic. A few ran toward the apartment building, but most followed a sidewalk that appeared to lead to a neighborhood close by. Dirk could feel the startled amazement of his friends as they surveyed the children.

Keiko was the first to find her voice. "So many different races—they're beautiful!" she said. "Every color of the rainbow!"

"Whoa!" Mateo said to no one in particular. "It's like a fantasy come to life."

"This is a time before the Merger." Nicci spoke the obvious.

"Guys, this is how it was *supposed* to be. Always. This is what we have to restore." Dirk hoped that the sight of so many children, so many *races,* was fueling a sense of purpose in the others the same way it was inside of him.

"Is restoring like *fixing* something? What are you trying to fix? Maybe I could help you."

A boy who looked to be about nine years of age stood before them. Keiko marveled that they had not even heard him climb the stairs. What she noticed first were his beautiful brown eyes, so different from the blue eyes that all children inhabiting the future possessed. His hair was more orange than red, and the freckles that peppered the bridge of his nose seemed to multiply and spread across his face the longer Keiko looked at him. His faded jeans, patched at the knees, were far too short, as the colored ribbing on his calf-high socks revealed, and his glasses were a bit too large for his petite round face. "I'm really good at fixing things. Ask anyone!" He smiled, first at Dirk, to whom he was directing his comments, and then at the others. His smile, though it defied explanation, captured each of them in the single gesture of goodwill.

Dirk crouched down to his knees. "You look like the kind of guy who *could* fix just about anything, buddy. But what we need to fix is a little more complicated than the kind of stuff you're probably used to working on. You live around here?"

"Yeah! Down there." the boy pointed toward the south end of the building. He grabbed Dirk's hand and pulled him through the others—beckoning for everyone to follow. "C'mon, I'll show you. Maybe you can meet Nana Ruth."

"I don't know that I want to meet anybody who lives in this heap," Mateo said under his breath. Nicci elbowed him and shot him a look that suggested he keep quiet.

When they arrived at a door marked 207, the boy knocked loudly. "Nana Ruth!" he called, "I'm home!"

"207?" Dirk questioned. "I thought this was the third floor."

"Oh, it is," the boy answered good-naturedly. He rapped on the door again, and then turned to face them. "Sometimes things just don't make sense, you know?"

The doorknob rattled and a bit of a struggle seemed to take place on the other side of the door before it opened. An elderly woman, tiny and quite fragile looking, stood before them. Her gray hair was braided and pinned in such a way that it crossed the top of her head in an arc. She wore a flowered cotton housedress and slippers. Her eyes were deep brown, like the boy's, and warm.

"Nana!" the boy called and threw his arms around the woman with such vigor that Dirk thought she might fall over, but she held her ground.

"Why, it appears my boy has brought friends home today," she said as she smoothed his hair with affection. "Would you like to come in?" She pulled the door back invitingly.

Dirk hesitated and looked at the others. He didn't see how this was going to help them find Michael Quinn. "Thanks," he said kindly, "but we really have to . . ."

"Stay *just* long enough to see this young man's room," said Keiko, marching past her friends and giving Dirk a wry smile.

"Awesome!" said the boy as he ran to his room to prepare it for visitors.

Dirk stood holding the screen door open as Nicci and Mateo sailed in. Mateo stopped to elbow him in the stomach. "Some *leader* you're turning out to be!" he said with a grin.

The visit lasted much longer than even Keiko had intended, but the boy had a way of captivating his audience. Everything from the tour of his tiny bedroom to the demonstrations of things he had fixed around the apartment was detailed with such energy and excitement that a genuine interest was subtly crafted in Dirk and his friends. Even Nana Ruth, who had surely heard and seen it all time and again, watched and listened in fascination. Before they knew it, the hustle and bustle from Nana's kitchen led to an evening meal for six that evoked a sense of family in all of them that settled as comfortably as dusk. As dinner dishes were cleared, Nicci strolled over to the only object in the apartment that retained any sense of splendor. Though she had never seen a piano before, Nicci easily recognized the instrument from the many books Lisa Tyrone had used to teach them.

"Oh, the piano!" cried Nana rushing in from the kitchen. "What a splendid idea. A sing-along would be the perfect way to cap off the evening. Yes?" She was already seating herself at the instrument when the boy burst forth in a rallying tune that soon found them parading around the living room following his lead. The concert ended nearly an hour later with Nana Ruth leading them in an old ballad. Keiko looked at the glowing faces around the room and wondered at how easily it had all come together. It seemed unlikely that a first meeting would bring forth such strong feelings, and yet there was no denying that everyone had let their guard down tonight. As they drew in close to sing a final chorus, a warmth filled Keiko—a result of the contentment her friends were feeling. Quite suddenly, then, she knew with certainty why the evening had moved ahead in just this way—and why she and her friends had become such eager and willing participants in it. "This is a taste of what we never had," she thought. And it was true. Robbed of their parents and hidden away from the merged society that surrounded them, none of them had a memory like this one to recall.

"Well," Nana said as she rose from the bench. "It's past someone's bedtime! I know it without even looking at the clock."

Dirk felt a small hand clasp his tightly. "Nana! I want *them* to tuck me in tonight. *Please!*"

Nana Ruth did not protest. She simply looked at Dirk questioningly. He nodded to the youngster. "Go get changed. We'll be there in a minute."

The four of them made quick work of cleaning up the kitchen under Nana Ruth's direction and then made their way into the boy's tiny bedroom. Their new friend was already lying down, and a reluctant yawn escaped him as they surrounded his bed.

"Thanks for staying." He said it with such sincerity that

they realized how much the evening had meant to him. "I . . . um . . . I don't really have a lot of friends over. I mean, Nana does the best she can, but this place isn't exactly where you bring kids from school. Most of them have houses, you know, and stuff, and . . . well, just thanks. That's all."

Dirk ruffled the boy's hair gently. "Listen, buddy, it was a great night for us, too. It's time for us to head on out though and for you to get some shut-eye."

"Don't forget to fix whatever it is that needs fixing."

"Yeah! We're gonna get right on that," Mateo said as he followed Dirk back into the living area.

Nicci and Keiko each gave the boy a kiss on the forehead. "Sweet dreams," the girls said in unplanned unison and giggles started up immediately. Nicci heard Mateo's voice and the sound of his opening the front door. "Time for us to go," she said softly. Keiko left the room with her and closed the door gently behind them. Dirk was saying his goodbye to Nana Ruth as they approached.

"Well, you've just made it such a memorable night. I can't thank you enough for coming!" Her lean body was eager to give them each a hug, and it appeared the woman was overjoyed to have the warm good-bye reciprocated. "Michael will be talking about this visit all week long!" she said with excitement.

"We'll remember it, too," said Dirk. "The little guy really . . ." He stopped mid-sentence. A look of disbelief in Nicci's eyes caught his attention at the same time the name registered in his ears. Keiko took a step backward. Her hand flew to her mouth in a vain effort to stifle the soft gasp that escaped.

Mateo poked his head back in the front door. "What's *with* you guys? I'm standin' out here and . . ." The silence told him something was terribly wrong.

Nana Ruth's eyes flickered. "What is it?" She took a handkerchief from her pocket and began to wind it nervously in her hands. "What's *wrong?*"

Dirk could not find his voice. "Did you . . . did you say *Michael? His name is Michael?"*

"Well, yes. Yes. I'm Ruth Quinn, and Michael is my grandson. His parents were killed last year in a terrible traffic accident. Why? What's wrong? Do you know something about his parents? The accident? Who *are* you?"

"Um . . . we . . . we're friends, Mrs. Quinn. That's all. We just . . . well, we've overstayed our welcome. We need to be going." Dirk rushed everyone out the door as quickly as possible. He felt guilty for leaving Nana Ruth with a host of unanswered questions, but what could they really tell her? No one spoke as Nicci swept them away to the downtown area where they found a local coffee shop that was nearly deserted.

"A KID! Michael Quinn is a kid!" Mateo burst out as they settled into a booth.

Nicci put a hand on his arm to quiet him. "We all were once, Matty."

"Yeah, sure! But they didn't tell us we'd be going *this* far into the past! They didn't tell us he'd be a *kid!* No! No! This can't be right. Nicci, something's wrong. You overshot the time thing."

"Mateo," she looked at him fiercely, "I did *not* mess this up. This is where we're supposed to be. This is *when* we're supposed to be."

"Then *why* didn't Madam tell us he was . . ."

"Because *I* would not have come." Keiko supplied the answer that silenced them all. "I've been struggling with Michael Quinn's fate and the role we are to play in it from the very beginning. If they had told us he was a child, I would have refused to merge with you. I would *never* have come if I had known. The Elders knew that." There was a long pause in the conversation.

Dirk sat quietly looking out the window as rain began to pour down. He had figured out what none of the others had, and there was no point in hiding it. "Guys, it's worse than you think." The intensity of his eyes paralyzed them. "Michael Quinn *dies* saving an old lady's life."

Nicci brought her hand to her mouth. She could suddenly feel her own pulse in her ears, and it was pounding away. *"Nana Ruth!"* she gasped.

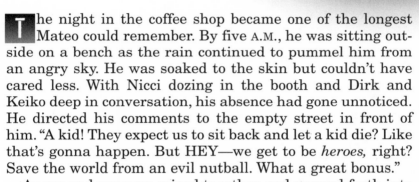

The night in the coffee shop became one of the longest Mateo could remember. By five A.M., he was sitting outside on a bench as the rain continued to pummel him from an angry sky. He was soaked to the skin but couldn't have cared less. With Nicci dozing in the booth and Dirk and Keiko deep in conversation, his absence had gone unnoticed. He directed his comments to the empty street in front of him. "A kid! They expect us to sit back and let a kid die? Like that's gonna happen. But HEY—we get to be *heroes,* right? Save the world from an evil nutball. What a great bonus."

Anger and sarcasm mixed together and spewed forth into the early morning. If Mrs. Morph and the others could hear him, if they were here right now, he would sure have some words for them. "I should never have trusted you!" he shouted aloud as raindrops hammered the street. Why was it that, despite his angry words, his heart was longing for Mrs. Morph to appear? His grimace gave way to a slight grin as he imagined her chastising him for sitting out in the rain.

Mateo spotted movement near the corner and tensed. He was well aware that Senator Broogue could be anywhere, but it was a dog that came trotting around the corner and approached him. Mateo relaxed instantly; he loved dogs! "Hey there, pup, what's up? You a Lassie-dog, huh?" Two strong but friendly barks rang forth. The collie placed her head on his knee and thumped her tail against the sidewalk. "Okay, so you know your breed. That's good. Where I come from they've sort of taken care of that for us, ya know? They want us all the same. And me and my buddies are tryin' to change that."

"Woof!" She wagged a tail and spun in a circle twice.

Mateo couldn't help but smile. "Oh! So you think it's a good idea for me and my pals to shake things up a little, eh?"

"WOOF! WOOF!" The dog stood on her hind legs and managed, with some difficulty, to walk a few steps forward and put one paw on Mateo's shoulder. For just a moment their eyes met, and the dog's eyes, so soulful, reminded Mateo that Lisa Tyrone had told them dogs were man's best friend. Of course, they'd never been allowed to have a dog. It would have been too great a risk. A dog, Lisa had explained again and again, could not be easily kept in hiding and would most likely give them all away at some point. The collie sat back on her haunches and rested her chin on Mateo's knee again. Her tail began to hit the sidewalk so hard that it actually made a noise. Then, she whined a bit and shook herself so that water flew from her coat in every direction.

"You cold, pooch? Yeah, me too, a little." The rain had slowed to more of a light drizzle, and daylight was breaking. By now, Dirk and Keiko had surely figured out what their next move should be. "Listen, I gotta go, okay? My friends are inside, and I know you aren't allowed in the coffee shop. See ya around, girl." Mateo headed inside without looking back.

The dog jumped up on the bench Mateo had vacated and sprawled across it. Her eyes never left the door through which he had disappeared. She gave the appearance of a loyal pet waiting for its owner.

"A DOG! Matty, we do NOT need a dog!" Dirk was digging through a toolbox for a wrench while the girls were putting serious muscle into scouring the kitchen of the two-bedroom apartment they now had for living quarters. The dog sat on her haunches just inside the door.

"But, Dirk, she followed us here. What am I supposed to do with her? Besides, she's real smart. Hey, watch this, you guys. Dog! *Catch this!*" Mateo tossed a round plastic liner from inside the toolbox into the air. It came down on the collie's head. She jumped back, sat again, and cocked her head to the side questioningly. The girls tried to muffle their laughter as Dirk pulled out the wrench and put his hands on his hips.

Mateo shrugged. "So . . . she's not so good with flying objects. Big deal. She might come in handy!"

A quick rap on the screen door sent the dog scurrying to Mateo's side. Michael Quinn's face poked into the screen. "Hey! A dog! You have Lassie. Awesome! He was inside the door and kneeling beside the dog in a fraction of an instant. Her tail thumped happily as Michael stroked her fur. He looked at Dirk. "Don't let the *super* find out about her, or you'll be in big trouble! *No Pets! It says so in the lease!*" Michael appeared to be imitating the voice of the building superintendent with whom he had apparently had past discussions regarding pets.

Nicci laughed at the young boy's imitation and walked over to him. "She's not our dog, Michael. I'm not sure if we'll keep her, but . . ."

"WOOF! WOOF!" The dog barked in protest, and Michael threw his arms around her neck. "You gotta keep her, guys. Nana Ruth and I have watched lots of old movies about Lassie. She always saves everyone, and you never know when you might need saving."

The irony of Michael's words was not lost on any of them. Dirk noted that Keiko remained in the kitchen—wiping out the interior of the cabinets. She did not come out to greet Michael. "Well, we'll think on the dog, buddy. Right now, though, I have to get busy. Mr. Edwards, the super—to you—agreed to let us do some work on your building in exchange for this apartment and a very small amount of cash. I don't want to lose my job on the first day, and Mrs. Perkins in 322 needs her sink looked at."

"Oh, she's a delightful woman!" Nana Ruth stood at the door, and Dirk immediately moved to open it. The dog's ears shot up, and she backed into Mateo's legs, emitting a low growl.

"Mrs. Quinn, come in, please," Dirk spoke apologetically. "I'm sorry about last night. It was late, and we hadn't secured housing. I guess I was pretty rude and . . ."

"Please—call me Nana Ruth—all of you. Everyone does." She wiped her hands on her apron. "I . . . umm . . . was wondering, Dirk, if you could help me move a dresser upstairs. I haven't cleaned behind it in ages."

"Sure." Dirk was happy to do something nice for the elderly woman after the fine meal she had cooked last night. "Matty and I will come right up."

"NO!" Her tone was sharp—just for a moment. Nicci noticed a panicked look in Nana's eyes, but it was gone almost as quickly as it had appeared. Keiko stepped out of the shadows of the small kitchen and into view for the first time. She was sensing that something was not quite right with Nana Ruth. The woman grasped Dirk's arm firmly and began leading him out the door. "I don't really need *two* of you. It's a small dresser. You'll be able to do the job alone, Dirk."

Without warning, the dog lunged forward—snarling ferociously and positioning herself between Nana Ruth and the now-released Dirk.

"What the . . . Matty, come and get this mutt!"

"Oh, it's all right. Unfamiliar face—I should have known better than to reach for you with your dog nearby." Nana Ruth held the door open for Dirk to walk through. "Thank you, dear, for agreeing to help me. Shall we go?"

Matty was reaching for the dog when suddenly she crouched low, facing Nana Ruth, and it became clear that she was going to jump. She growled viciously and leaped, but she sailed through the air and collided with nothing. Nana Ruth evaporated before their eyes.

"BROOGUE!" Dirk shouted.

"Nana!" Michael cried out and ran forward. "She disappeared! I saw her and then she was just . . . gone."

"Oh, boy!" said Mateo, patting Dirk on the shoulder. "I think we got more trouble than a dog, buddy. But—hey—at least *you* get to be in charge!"

By late afternoon, Dirk had managed to wipe Michael's mind clear of the incident with Senator Broogue and his impersonation of Nana Ruth. He had not, however, managed to fix Mrs. Perkins' sink. It had been Keiko who had successfully found and stopped the leak while Nicci and Mateo had gone shopping for food and miscellaneous household supplies.

Conversation around the dinner table in their small, furnished apartment focused on a name for the dog. Keiko welcomed that topic in place of a discussion about Michael Quinn's fate. She found herself wishing there could be hundreds of dogs to name, in fact. There was no question of the collie's status after she saved Dirk from falling into the Senator's grasp. The name, however, was proving much more difficult.

"I like *Buttons*," Nicci said for the fourth time. "It's so sweet."

"You are *not* naming my dog Buttons, Nicci! Now stop with the cutesy names. Did you see how she went after the Senator? Imagine if it had been *me* he was tryin' to snatch. She probably would have torn him limb from limb right then and there. Huh, girl?" The collie responded with a loud and steady bark. Resting her head on Mateo's knee and pumping her tail hard against the floor had become a habit, and she did so now with great enthusiasm.

"What about *Tiger*, 'cause she's got that killer instinct, *or Leo*, like a lion?" proposed Dirk.

Keiko had been relatively quiet, content to listen to the

others toss out ideas, but this was too much. "Leo? Dirk, you do not name a girl dog Leo! What about Cookie or Muffin?"

Mateo smacked his forehead in disbelief. "You girls are NUTS! It's a wonder dogs who get named by girls don't just run out and throw themselves under cars and end it all right then and there—just so they don't have to listen to their ridiculous names! A name has to *mean* something. It should sorta show the dog's personality. Her name's *Champion*. You can call her Champ if you want to—but none of those *honey-sweetie* nicknames. You girls got that?"

Nicci grimaced. "Matty, you talk about us and our names. Whoever heard of a *girl* dog named Champion?"

The collie lifted her head and barked as if to say "enough is enough." Then, she rested her head back on Mateo's knee and thumped the floor with her tail once again. He patted her head and scratched behind her ears. "She's a tom-boy kinda dog, so the name's okay. It's Champion!" He said it with such finality that they all knew the discussion had ended. The collie was now a full-fledged member of their group. Later that night, she stationed herself on a rug between Dirk's bed and Mateo's. Eventually, though, she found her way onto Mateo's bed where she rooted under covers and kicked and rolled so much that by the end of the night he was on the floor, and she had the entire bed to herself.

A late morning breakfast brought nervous chatter from everyone. Nicci felt sure they were all doing their best to avoid talking about Michael. She knew she was. Each time she thought of the sandy-haired boy, she was overwhelmed with the task that had befallen them. How *could* it be that one person's life could be so instrumental in shaping the future? Did people walk around day to day with an awareness of their power as individuals? She doubted it. She knew she had never considered the enormity of it. Michael Quinn, and what they knew about him, had certainly changed all of that. She tensed as Dirk rested both elbows on the table and began to speak. "Listen, guys, I think we oughta . . ."

Keiko rose abruptly and headed to the bedroom she and Nicci shared. She avoided all eye contact. "Excuse me. I am not feeling well."

"Keiko!" Dirk's frustration was evident. "We have to talk about this. You can't just avoid it day after day. You're gonna have to sit down and deal with it."

And that's when something snapped. The serene demeanor, so much a part of Keiko's personality, was replaced with a ferocious intensity as she whirled around to face her friends. It was Dirk, though, to whom she addressed her comments. *"Deal with it?* Well, that's an interesting way of putting things, isn't it, Dirk? Why are you saying it that way? Why not call it like it is?" Without realizing it, Keiko had begun shouting. "We're talking about *killing* someone—a *child!* How *dare* you criticize me for not wanting to sit in on the planning meeting!"

Dirk stood at the table and faced her; it felt like they were adversaries. What did she think—that this was *easy* for him? "We are not talking about killing anyone, Keiko. We're talking about allowing the natural order of events . . ."

"Excuse me if I don't stay for your rationalizations, Dirk. Who *are* you? It feels like I don't even know you anymore. You fully intend to let that little boy die just because it was *supposed* to happen. Says WHO?"

Nicci could tell Dirk needed help. She also knew that if she entered the conversation, she would be putting her friendship with Keiko on the line. So be it. "Says Madam and Dr. Pan—all of them, Keiko! You think they would lie to us about something like this?" She walked over to Keiko and placed a hand on the girl's shoulder. "You can't tell me you truly believe they would ask us to . . ."

Keiko swept Nicci's hand from her shoulder. "Get your hands off me, Nicci! They didn't tell us Michael Quinn would be a *child!*"

Silence.

Nicci was stunned . . . and hurt. Keiko could see it in her eyes and sense it. But the truth was that she didn't care.

Mateo approached Keiko from the other side. "Look, Keiko. You're right, okay? None of us considered he would be a kid. But it doesn't *change* anything. The Merger was never meant to happen. Broogue knew that if he saved Michael Quinn's life as a boy, the kid would go on to impact history in such a way that the Senator's ideas would be readily accepted by world leaders. *Broogue's* the bad guy here, not us."

Dirk came out from behind the table, too, but removing the barrier did not seem to alter the distance he felt from Keiko right now. He reached out and took her hands in his. "Keiko, listen to Matty. *We* aren't the bad guys."

She wrenched her hands from his with unexpected force and the tears spilled forth. "I will *not* kill a child. I will not stand willingly by and let a child die. I cannot do it, Dirk. I WON'T!" And then she fell into him and sobbed as though the very life were draining out of her.

Champ, who had been lying on the ground with her head in her paws, snapped to attention suddenly and barked. Dirk and his friends followed her gaze to the door. Michael Quinn stood just outside the screen. He appeared to have heard at least some of what had been said—though exactly how much was anyone's guess. He looked at Dirk as if he no longer knew him and backed away from the door. "Are you guys gonna hurt someone? Are you gonna hurt *me?*"

Some fast talk, a trip to the park, and a big ice cream cone were Mateo and Nicci's solution to the current Michael Quinn dilemma. Meanwhile, Dirk divided his time between repairs on both the building and Keiko, neither of which went well. What Dirk did not know was that Senator Broogue was lurking nearby. He was aware of much of what was going on with the teens, and his prediction that Keiko would be the weak link was proving correct. Defeating them was going to be child's play.

His attempt to capture Dirk the day before had been nothing more than a show— something to make them all believe their leader was still his primary target. He had never thought to succeed in that attempt, though if he had been successful that would have been acceptable, too. Adrenaline flowed through him like lightning, and his heart rate increased each time he thought of what would happen once he had Dirk's abilities poured into his own. "Soon," he told himself, "very soon it will be finished."

The big surprise yesterday had been the dog. Where had it come from? The Senator was not used to surprises, and that one could have proven disastrous if his plan to take Dirk had been critical. The dog's apparent loyalty to Dirk and his friends troubled Senator Broogue—but obviously not enough—for he did not allow himself to dwell on the issue as long as he should have.

The rest of the week played out rather calmly. The charade of Dirk's being "Mr. Fix-It" was kept up by Mateo, Nicci, and Keiko—who fixed practically everything when the building superintendent wasn't around. And in the evening, if Dirk had a job before dinner, Michael Quinn went with him and successfully counseled him through repairs on everything from drywall and electrical work to plumbing and air conditioners. Nearly every night, dinner involved both Nana Ruth and Michael. Keiko, working against the best interests of everyone, initiated these gatherings despite Dirk's attempt to dissuade her.

"Keiko's got it in her head," Mateo said during a lunch meeting with Nicci and Dirk, "that the more time we spend with the kid, the more likely we are to keep him from . . . well, you know."

Dirk's frustration with Keiko knew no limit at this point. He had taken to meeting with the others at lunch to plan around her. He hated doing it, but he thought it best that she have no knowledge of what the plan was going to be on the night of Michael's death. She *had* to be present. Dirk instinctively knew that they all four would need to be there. He just had not yet figured out a way to keep her from saving Michael's life. "This is hard on all of us, Matty! But we have to trust Madam and the others. We have to let nature take its course."

Champ barked her agreement and chased her tail. Dirk knew it was easier to talk about letting Michael die than it was going to be to actually let it happen when the time came. For each moment Michael spent following them around, singing with them at the piano, or laughing at their antics around the dinner table, the boy was becoming more and more a part of them. Keiko's plan was working.

Nana Ruth had made an especially fine pecan pie for

dessert that evening. Nicci and Mateo had eagerly responded to her request for volunteers to top off her carefully sliced pieces with whipped cream, and Champ, rarely far from Mateo's side, had cheerfully followed them into the kitchen. "Bad news, Nana Ruth," Mateo said as he spooned some cream artfully onto a second piece of pie. He offered a finger of the delicious cream to the collie when no one was looking. "The whipping cream well has run dry, and I've only done two pieces."

Nana looked unperturbed as she skillfully removed her apron. "Well, that was my poor planning indeed, Matty. I can remedy it, though. Mr. Thompson's drugstore is only a few blocks away, and he keeps a cooler. I'll bet he's got whipped cream in there!" She reached for her purse, and instantaneously Nicci began to tingle all over. Champ cocked her head sideways and emitted a low growl.

"Hey! Nana, why don't I . . ."

Nicci grabbed Mateo's wrist with considerable force. Her intense gaze told him to say no more. This was the moment they had been waiting for.

"Er . . . uh . . . I mean why don't you go to that store down on Jefferson Street instead? I hear they have better prices." Mateo felt sick to his stomach, for that was not what he had intended to say at all. He had been about to offer to accompany her to the store.

"Why, don't be silly, Matty." Nana laughed. "That's Mr. Bink's store. His prices are inflated. He should be ashamed, and I've told him so. Besides, he always flirts with me when I go in there, and I'll have none of it." She elbowed Nicci on her way out the apartment's back door. "I've told him *that,* too," she said, stepping out onto the landing.

The silence in the kitchen settled heavily on Nicci and Mateo as they heard Nana Ruth making her way down the back staircase. Neither spoke. Part of their plan required Nicci to have visited the future, quickly, to gather a few bits

of information about this night. She had not stayed long for
fear the Senator would come after her, so she had gathered
only sketchy details. For example, she had not been able to
determine what it was that would lead Nana Ruth outside
on the fateful night. Now, she knew. She reminded herself
that Nana would have been in this kitchen running out of
whipped cream even if they had not been here. "We are *not*
the cause of this," she told herself sternly. If only her heart
could embrace what her mind was telling her. She looked at
her friend fleetingly and then down to the floor. "Matty,
there may not be much time. We've got to go now."

Terribly discordant piano keys indicated that Michael and
Dirk were trying once again to bang out "Heart and Soul"
under Keiko's guidance. Nicci and Mateo burst through the
swinging kitchen door a bit too forcefully. The piano keys
stopped. "Dirk," Nicci tried to retain her composure, "Nana
Ruth has gone to the drugstore . . . for whipped cream."
Keiko's head shot up abruptly, and her dark eyes grew wide.
It sounded almost as if Nicci was speaking to Dirk in a
code—giving him a message that Michael would not understand.

Dirk had tried earnestly to prepare himself to behave like
a true leader when this moment came. Now, it was here, and
all he wanted to do was hide somewhere and let someone
else call the shots. Surely the insides of a great leader had
never turned to jelly the way his had just now. He tried to
shake the feeling that everything was riding on his decisions tonight, but it settled on him heavily.

"She's gone out by herself!" Michael was concerned. "Nana
doesn't see that well at night. I always go with her to the
drugstore!" He was out the door in a second, and to everyone's surprise, Keiko didn't move to stop him. She sat like a
statue—her face impassive.

"Keiko," said Nicci, deciding the pressure had best come
from her. "We really have to . . ."

"I want our world to see us the way Michael does," Keiko's quiet voice resonated with determination. "His protests against the war in college had nothing to do with supporting a Merged race. The Senator brought that to fruition; he *used* Michael's love of humanity and drive for peace for a terrible purpose. If we allow it to continue, the true Michael Quinn, who he is and was and what he believed in, will be lost forever. It has taken me some time, but I have come to this conclusion."

It was all Dirk could do not to grab her in his arms and kiss her like he was sure she'd never been kissed before. She must have sensed the passionate thought because she looked at him with mock surprise and cocked an eyebrow.

He grinned and mouthed the word "later."

A loud clap of thunder intensified the need for action. "All right. The train's leaving folks. Let's go!" Nicci summoned them to her, and Champion, sensing that they were going somewhere, rushed to Mateo's side. Nicci engulfed them in a golden aura, and a moment later they appeared on the dark street outside of Thompson's drugstore. Inside the store, an armed robbery was in progress.

CHAPTER 21

The winds were strong and menacing as Nicci and her friends appeared behind a hedgerow across the street from Thompson's drugstore. There was no sign of Nana Ruth, though they guessed she was already inside and that Michael would be arriving shortly. The big question in all of their minds was spoken by Mateo. "So where's Broogue?"

"It doesn't really matter," Dirk's voice rang with conviction. "We know what we have to do. Nicci, you still think you can pull this off?"

"I've been practicing, Dirk. I can manage. You just have to let me know when."

For the first time, Keiko was aware that there had obviously been discussions she had missed out on. "What's going on? What's Nicci going to do?" Dirk's eyes were closed tightly. He seemed to be concentrating intently, so Keiko decided not to force the issue.

Dirk was, in fact, using a tremendous amount of mental energy. His conscious mind had left his body and moved inside the drugstore—not only to see what was happening, but to determine if Senator Broogue was there. Despite the fact that Nicci had visited the future and prepared Dirk for what would happen in the drugstore, he was shocked to see a masked man in the store holding a gun on Nana Ruth. An open bag, which Mr. Thompson was nervously filling with money, lay on the counter. "You got more than this, old man!" The robber wasn't asking—he was telling. "You find some more money fast, or Grandma here is goin' to bite the dust."

Even though Dirk knew that history would protect Nana Ruth on this night, it was difficult to watch her being held

by this creep. If he had been present physically rather than
mentally, he wasn't sure he could have stayed out of the way.
He stretched out mentally, groping for the Senator. Still
nothing. Curious. Where was he? Why wasn't he here yet?

Dirk decided the best course of action, for now, was to
head back to his friends, and just as he prepared to do so, he
sensed Michael coming on the run less than a block away;
Senator Broogue's mental presence surrounded the boy.
Dirk launched himself back into his physical body immediately, and his eyes shot open so quickly the others were startled. "They're coming!" He told them. "Michael is hoofing it
down the street pretty fast," he motioned with his finger.
"Broogue's all over him. There's a robbery in the store just
like we expected. The guy has a gun on Nana Ruth, and he's
getting money from Thompson." Dirk pulled out a ski mask
and some dark clothes from a small duffel bag and tossed
them to Keiko. "Put these on, Keiko, fast!"

"What? Dirk I . . ."

Nicci's voice was filled with impatience. She shoved Keiko
deeper into the shadows so the girl could change clothes.
"Just DO this, Keiko! You're going to impersonate the robber! Quick now . . . I'll fill you in on what's going to happen
next, but you have to hurry!"

Champ began running in circles around Mateo and growl-
ing ferociously. "It's okay, girl. We know he's coming. We'll be
okay." Mateo's voice was the only calm thing about him just
now.

"Matty, listen. You know what to do, right?" Dirk's voice
was all business.

"Yeah, Dirk. I got it. But I don't understand where we're
gonna get another Michael. We have two Nana Ruths—me
and the real one. We have two gunmen—Keiko and the real
one. But where are we gonna get a *second* Michael Quinn?"

Dirk punched his shoulder, "Trust me, my friend. He'll be
there when we need him."

Nicci and Keiko rejoined the others—Keiko looking surprisingly threatening in her black garb and with a gun of
her own. "She knows the game plan," Nicci said to Dirk
with a nod. Suddenly, a scream shot through the dark of
night. Nana Ruth was being dragged out of the store by the
gunman.

"NOW, Nicci, it's got to be NOW!" At once, Dirk assaulted
the Senator's mind with an intense series of quick jabbing
probes that were intended to distract him while Nicci seamlessly transported her three friends, as well as the Senator,
into what Madam called a *twin reality*. Simply put, a *twin
reality* was nothing more than the backdrop of a specific
moment in time—almost like the scenery for a play. In this
case, Nicci had created a sort of static "bubble"—a place
apart from the natural flow of time—and replicated the
scene outside of the drugstore on the night Michael Quinn
was shot. Dirk's entire plan hinged on tricking the Senator
into believing he was still outside the *real* Thompson's drugstore. If their enemy could be kept in this twin reality long
enough, a pivotal moment in history—Michael Quinn's
death—would happen in real time just as it was intended.
And if the Senator failed to save Michael's life, the plan for
a merging of races would never come to be.

As the twin reality took shape, Dirk leveled a final painful
strike against the Senator, who had been retaliating with
several forceful mental blows of his own. The plan worked.
Nothing in the Senator's mind indicated that he had noticed
Nicci's displacement of him from real time into the twin
reality. Dirk marveled at how Nicci's skills had improved; try
as he might, he could barely sense when the shift occurred,
and *he* knew it was happening. They were still outside the
store—or what appeared to be the store. Keiko, dressed as
the robber, held the gun on Mateo in his guise as Nana Ruth.
He struggled against her, just as the real Nana would no
doubt have done, but Keiko held him threateningly.

"NANA!" Michael's shout of fear filled their ears and laid their hearts to waste. Senator Broogue's physical outline could be seen standing just a few feet behind the boy.

Keiko was troubled—where had the boy come from? If the real Michael Quinn was going to be shot, tonight, in *real* time—who was the boy running toward her in this twin reality? Was this, somehow, the *real* Michael Quinn? Were her friends trying to trick her into allowing Michael to die? She pushed the thought away. While she was changing into the gunman attire, Nicci had assured her that, despite what her eyes told her, she would *not* be shooting at Michael Quinn tonight. Keiko was aware of what she had to do; she could not allow herself to become distracted. She had to fire the gun at this boy.

As Michael Quinn came within a few feet of his grand-mother, Senator Broogue stepped out of the shadows and pulled the boy forcefully to his side—protecting him from the bullet that should have been fired. Tonight, though, there was a delay. It was less than a second, perhaps less than a millisecond, but it *was* a delay. Keiko hesitated to fire, just as her friends had expected she would, and that moment of hesitation alerted the Senator that things were not as they should be. Why had the gunman hesitated to fire? Senator Broogue peered into the gunman's mind and discovered Keiko Tan hiding behind the mask. He had been deceived! His rage rang out loud and long in the night. He shoved Michael from him and moved towards her—and that's when she finally managed to pull the trigger. She screamed, dropped the weapon to the ground, and was swept out of the twin reality before Senator Broogue could harm her. The Senator cried out in fury again—launching himself out of the twin reality and back into real time. Ironically, he abandoned one Michael Quinn in the path of a bullet while hoping desperately to prevent a different Michael Quinn from ever being shot.

Mateo was stunned by Keiko's abrupt and unexpected departure. He reminded himself, though, that Dirk had remained tight-lipped about the plan all the way along—insisting that none of them know more than was absolutely necessary. "If I can't keep Broogue distracted enough mentally, I want to be sure that none of you knows enough to put the entire plan at risk. If he probes your minds and discovers any details, it'll all be over for us. You're just going to have to trust me." Those were his words to Mateo and Nicci in the final planning session held just a few days earlier, and they hadn't argued.

Mateo resumed his natural appearance and rushed to Michael Quinn, who was lying in the street. He pulled the boy into his lap and gasped when the boy's body morphed into that of his best friend.

"Whoa! Dirk! How did you manage to . . ." Mateo stopped in mid-sentence as Dirk's body shuddered.

"Matty, I'm trying to heal this, but it's pretty torn up. I don't know if I can stay conscious. I think you better get Keiko. I'm going to need her to . . ."

"You're trying to heal! Heal what? And since when do you have *our* abilities? Dirk, when you hold back information, you *really* hold it back—*if* ya know what I mean!" Dirk's body trembled, and he managed a half grin that turned to a grimace of pain. Mateo put his hand against his friend's chest and felt a sea of liquid. Instinctively, he drew his arm back and thrust his hand from the shadows. The streetlight revealed that it was covered in deep red blood. "Dirk! You *took* the bullet! NICCI!" He called her name with urgency. "You better get us out of here—and fast!"

Keiko rejoiced as Nicci pulled her out of the twin reality. It was like leaving behind a terrible nightmare. The Senator had looked at her with such hate that she did not want to imagine what might have happened if he had reached her before she departed. She had reappeared with Nicci, in real time, but they were no longer outside the drugstore. Keiko did not know where they were, in fact, and she didn't really care. The enormity of what she had done was becoming real to her.

"Nicci, I fired the gun—I kept telling myself that I had to—and I did. But it was so dark, and Senator Broogue was so . . . and then I fired . . . but I don't know if I . . ."

Nicci hugged her friend for a moment before speaking. "Keiko, I told you before—I promise—you did *not* shoot Michael Quinn."

Relief ballooned inside Keiko, but it was short-lived. The thought struck her almost immediately that Michael *had* been shot tonight in real time—outside of the twin reality. "Nicci, take me to him, PLEASE! I won't save him, I promise. I could ease the suffering, though. I could help him through it, make it so much easier." The thought of little Michael and Nana Ruth suffering together in the night was eating away at her insides.

"Sweetie, you *think* you wouldn't save his life . . . but you *would*. You wouldn't know when to stop, Keiko. Besides— there's someone else who may need your help right now."

The timbre of Nicci's voice was serious. Enough so that Keiko knew there was something more that had been kept from her. "What do you mean Nicci? Who needs me?"

"Keiko, if that bullet you fired made contact with a body tonight, it wasn't Michael Quinn's. It was *Dirk's.*"

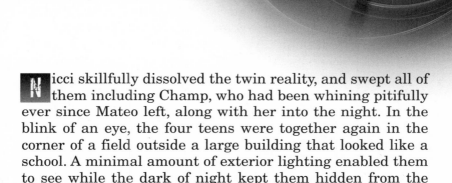

icci skillfully dissolved the twin reality, and swept all of them including Champ, who had been whining pitifully ever since Mateo left, along with her into the night. In the blink of an eye, the four teens were together again in the corner of a field outside a large building that looked like a school. A minimal amount of exterior lighting enabled them to see while the dark of night kept them hidden from the view of strangers.

One look at Dirk stole Keiko's breath. The gaping wound, his face so pale. And the blood—how could a human body hold so much blood?

"He's been unconscious for the last few minutes," Mateo explained worriedly. Champ whined nervously, running from Dirk to Mateo and back again. At last, Mateo grabbed the collie and held her close. "Easy girl," he said calmly as he rubbed her sable coat. Mateo was covered in Dirk's blood, too; clearly, his attempts to stop the bleeding had not even slowed it.

"Dirk? Dirk, I'm here." Keiko gently brushed his cheeks with her hands. His eyelashes fluttered, and he tried to grin. He wanted to say something clever, but the pain of the gunshot had been more than he had bargained for. The best he could do was grunt a soft "Hey there, Florence Nightingale." She took his hand for a brief moment and smiled. There was so much she wanted to say, but for now her eyes did all of the talking.

As if on cue, and not unexpectedly, Senator Broogue appeared in a gust of wind just a few feet from them. He was cradling Michael Quinn in his arms. The little boy's eyes

were closed, and Keiko sensed, immediately, that his heart
was failing.

"Help him . . . *please.*" The Senator looked at her imploringly. His voice spoke with a quality of tenderness and com-
passion she could not have imagined. "The empathic ability
I possess does not extend to anyone beyond myself," he
explained. He looked toward Dirk, who had struggled to
raise his head. As Dirk surveyed the scene before him, he
realized that Michael Quinn was the one person the Senator
could take with him through time. Madam had said there
was an exception, and of course the Senator had wisely chosen Michael—probably for just this type of situation. "Your
plan worked very well, Mr. Tyrone," the Senator appraised.
I was distracted by you just long enough."

"Michael." Keiko spoke his name in a whisper. Her mind
filled with images of the boy singing with them at the piano,
climbing into his bed, carrying Dirk's toolbox. The Senator
saw the images, too, and accentuated them until Keiko was
nearly in a trance. She walked toward the boy.

"Keiko, you can't!" Nicci warned.

The Senator offered the boy up to her. "He is the *key* to a
world of peace. *Save him!* Do what you were born to do—
heal!" He regarded the others. "Don't you see what the
Merger has done? Racial strife has ended. How many lives
have been saved from wars never fought over *race?* How
many gangs never formed? How many . . ."

"It's a *sham,* Senator. You haven't achieved racial harmony; you've simply hidden what's really underneath and
inside of people." Nicci could see that he really believed he
was doing the right thing. It was amazing how a person
could get so twisted up inside.

"Can't you see what's happened?" Mateo spoke in earnest.
"It's like the pain and anger—the loss you dealt with as a
kid—got multiplied in your head or something. I mean, it's
one thing to want to make the world a better place . . . but

look how you went about doing it. Look at the *cost*. You destroyed your friendships. Worse yet, you took a major piece of what makes people unique and erased it—you stole physical identity from an entire world! People's physical differences can be a reason to come together—as well as to pull apart. You took away the chance for people to make that decision for themselves!"

"Uuhhhhh!" Dirk closed his eyes. His head fell back and hit the ground and the blood began to flow quickly across his chest again. Keiko turned to look back at him. Michael Quinn's eyelids fluttered; he opened his eyes.

"Di . . . did . . . you," he spoke in shallow, halting gasps. Keiko could not bear it.

"Keiko, you've got to help Dirk—NOW!" Mateo stomped his foot, and Champ barked twice and growled.

"He's a *child!*" The Senator's voice was edged with persuasion. "Just a moment or two to ease the pain. Then, you can help your friend."

Michael looked at Keiko again. "Did y . . . you . . . guys . . . ever . . . fi . . . fix . . ."

Senator Broogue eyed Mateo and Nicci who were distracted both by Michael's words and Dirk's struggle to hang on to life. With Dirk unable to protect them or even to come to their aid, Senator Broogue leveled his psychic attack with no warning at all—placing each of them in a recurring nightmare that would literally paralyze them with fear until their minds eventually collapsed from the strain. He grabbed Keiko's arm, pulling her forcefully to him and shoving her hands to Michael's chest. He held her there with every ounce of his strength and entered her mind. *"Now, healer, you will HEAL! Heal this child while your boyfriend bleeds to death and your friends become lifeless shells! You, my dear, are the weak link in the chain. Do you know that? You've failed everyone miserably, except for me."* His words were well-chosen and intentional, serving, he hoped, to create mounting

despair in the girl. He had waited a long time for this! He
was going to make sure he enjoyed it.

Keiko fought against him, but she could not ignore his
mental suggestion that she use her empathic abilities to
save Michael. He was forcing her to save the boy and to
ignore Dirk's condition. Either Dirk or Michael could have
lived tonight, she realized, and Dirk had known all along it
might come to this. He had placed his life in jeopardy knowing that it could come to a forced-choice situation. He had
gambled that, in the end, she would save *him*. And she
would have, she knew that now. True, she had hesitated for
a moment, distracted by Michael's smallness, his innocence.
She had been thinking that she could ease his suffering and
save Dirk as well. But reason would have won out in the
end! She *would* have made the right choice . . . but she had
hesitated. Now, as her healing power flowed into Michael
Quinn, Keiko Tan realized that it was too late for second
chances.

The Senator was immeasurably pleased with himself. So
much so, in fact, that he had not realized there was still one
member of Keiko's party who was still free to act.
Champion's arrival on top of him was followed by his sharp
cry of alarm. She pinned the startled Senator to the ground
and gave a sharp bark. Dirk stirred slightly. The collie's eyes
caught his for just an instant, but there was something
there—something familiar. He touched her mind and was
amazed by what he discovered. Even in his weakened state,
Dirk was able to recognize the urgency of the thoughts
directed toward him from the dog, and he responded—using
the last of his mental strength to create a merger between
Champ and Senator Broogue.

She did not know what was happening or how, but Champ
was keeping the Senator busy—providing Keiko with a
chance to set things right. She ran to Dirk's motionless body,

knelt beside it, and began drawing the pain away. He was losing consciousness. Was she too late? She leaned over him and tilted his head up. Placing her hands on each side of his face, she kissed him the way she had always dreamed of kissing him. The pain and the agony from within his body began to pour into hers at an alarming rate, threatening to steal her own life, but still she held on, her lips firmly locked against his. She was not going to lose him after all of this.

Dirk's conscious mind began to clear so that he realized what was happening. He worried that Keiko was taking on too much. Everyone had limits, including her. He was afraid for her safety, but at the same time desperate for the healing she was offering. He wanted her to stop, but he wanted her to continue. Finally, it struck him; he realized exactly *how* she was restoring him and that put things quickly into perspective. "They never interrupt a doctor in the middle of an operation," he reminded himself. "Surely she knows the extent of her own abilities." Then he smiled and let her go right on kissing him. Sleeping Beauty had nothing on him.

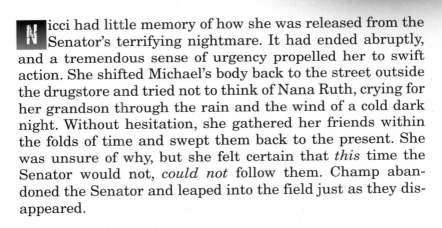

icci had little memory of how she was released from the Senator's terrifying nightmare. It had ended abruptly, and a tremendous sense of urgency propelled her to swift action. She shifted Michael's body back to the street outside the drugstore and tried not to think of Nana Ruth, crying for her grandson through the rain and the wind of a cold dark night. Without hesitation, she gathered her friends within the folds of time and swept them back to the present. She was unsure of why, but she felt certain that *this* time the Senator would not, *could not* follow them. Champ abandoned the Senator and leaped into the field just as they disappeared.

Sitting on an outcropping of rock in the hills high above their city, Dirk and his friends relaxed in the sun. Their hearts were heavy over the loss of Michael's life, yet they all agreed the Senator's distorted timeline was a perversion of all that was good in Michael. "Maybe," Dirk said thoughtfully, "the timing of life and death is not meant for us to understand." His friends nodded in agreement but remained quiet. They were waiting for explanations. Upon reappearing in the present, they had expected to be greeted by the Elders, and Dirk had a lot of explaining to do when Madam and her colleagues did not appear.

"Look guys," he said nervously, "I don't know that there's any great way to say this, so I'm just going to say it. The Elders aren't coming back—ever. They're gone."

His announcement was met with silence. None of his friends looked him in the eye.

"We wondered," Keiko said finally, "when you were meeting with them alone, if they might be revealing something like that."

"Setting the timeline right again could mean all kinds of possible changes," Nicci said. "I knew that—I just didn't want to think about it."

Mateo scratched behind Champ's ears. "They stuck around for so many years to make sure we had a shot at correcting the Merger. Maybe giving us that chance cost them everything in the end."

"If they had told us, the emotional strain would have been . . ." Keiko thought of kindly Dr. Pan's beaming face and said no more.

Dirk sighed and rested his head in his hands. When he looked up again, they were all waiting. "The Elders aren't here, guys, because during the merger between the seven of us—they each gave me some of their abilities." Matty's face revealed what he was thinking, but Dirk said it for him. "Yes, Matty, I used Mrs. Morph's ability to take on Michael's appearance."

"We knew the goal of Dirk's plan," Nicci spoke to Keiko, who had been involved in none of the planning meetings, "was to distract Broogue long enough for events to play out as they were supposed to with the *real* Michael in *real* time. That's why he had me create a twin reality."

"It took all of us, working together, to make the twin reality convincing," Mateo explained to Keiko, but then he looked at Dirk. "You couldn't tell us that you had some of the Elders' abilities for fear Broogue would find out! Right?"

Dirk's nod indicated Mateo was correct. "Madam's ability allowed me to move, as Michael, within the twin reality so that I could time my appearance on the street to coincide with the Senator's arrival once Nicci displaced him from real time. And Dr. Pan's ability kept me alive after I was shot—until I started losing consciousness. Then, you" he looked at Keiko, "you . . . uhhh sorta came over and . . . you know." His face reddened, and she reached for his hand.

"Oh, we know, Dirk!" Mateo said good-naturedly. "When Nicci and I came outta Broogue's festival of screams, you two were the first thing we saw. It was hard to tear our-selves away from all that romance, but then I saw that my girl here"—he ruffled Champ's coat—"had knocked Broogue over, and something *strange* was happening with the two of them!"

Nicci drew in a breath, "I noticed it, too, Matty! It was like . . . well, I don't know! It was like they were frozen in a bat-tle of wills. Neither of them was moving for a minute, but you could feel a struggle. That dog is amazing!"

Dirk could no longer suppress his laughter. When he had touched Champ's mind, her secret had been discovered, and he had immediately facilitated a merging of her mind with the Senator's. *That* was the strange battle his friends had sensed. Dirk looked at the dog lying near Mateo and grinned. "You want to tell them?" he asked the collie.

Champ rolled over on her back with her feet in the air and suddenly she *spoke.* "Awww geez! Ya dragged it outta me! I suppose it's okay, though, because this girl ain't never been one to keep secrets. If ya know what I mean."

Mateo jumped to his feet. "TEACH! It's *you!* I thought you couldn't travel back in time. Madam said the three of you couldn't . . ."

Nicci couldn't help but interrupt. Her mind was racing. "Are the others here, too? Madam? Madam!"

"Dr. Pan?" Keiko called excitedly. "Where is the doctor?"

"Calm down, everybody, calm down! They're both right here in the ole noggin with me, but they can't talk to ya like yours truly." The collie flipped back over onto her stomach. Mrs. Morph barked sharply once and then addressed Madam Moment, who could neither be seen nor heard because the Elders were all sharing the consciousness of the dog. "Margie, ya don't gotta be such a smartypants all the time. I *know* you told me so, but let's just remember *who's* in the driver's seat nowadays. Okay, kiddos, settle down and this girl will lay things on the line, shoot from the hip, not pull any punches, and get to the bottom of things for ya— 'cause that's the kinda girl I am."

"Teach, will you change back into yourself? I'd kinda like to see you."

"No can do, Matty, no can do. With this girl what ya see is what ya get these days. Ya see, kids, when we joined with you that day, we gave up some good stuff to Dirk, and we can't get it back on accounta it was given of our own free will and all. We was *supposed* to offer him everything and let him take what he wanted." The collie's ears drooped—leaving her looking rather sheepish. "Well, with me and Matty, it was kinda hard, ya know, sayin' goodbye to the big lug and all. So I sorta cheated a little bit. I ain't never been one for goin' strictly by the rules—if ya know what I mean. So I sorta kept a little transformin' power, ya know. I was always kinda fonda Lassie—how she was always so loyal to her boy and all—so I took this form for keeps!"

Nicci thought she understood. "So after Dirk took what he could from all of you . . ."

Mrs. Morph barked again and interrupted Nicci's thoughts. "Well, Margie figured out I was holdin' back so the three of us had a little, shall we say *heated discussion*. In the middle of it, you guys started to take off for the past, and, well, what was a girl like me ta do? I just sorta laid things on the line, and Margie finally bought in. The Doc—he's easy—it's Margie that wears ya down somethin' awful over *details!* Geez-o-Pete! So anyway, Margie and the Doc traveled on a stream of Dirk's consciousness right into the noggin of yours truly!" She looked at Dirk and wagged her tail. "You was so busy siftin' through our abilities, ya never even noticed."

"Actually," Dirk smiled, "I did sense something a little strange when *your* abilities were spilling through, Mrs. Morph, and I wondered if maybe . . ."

Mrs. Morph cut him off. "Ya *didn't* notice a thing, kid." She looked at the others. "This here is one crafty gal, kiddos. Nothin' gets past this girl. You can bank on that—I'm here ta tell ya. So anyways, we were all kinda in here together, got it? Then, Margie told me how to ride the wave of Nicci's time shift to the past—she said we could ride along safely if Nicci was doin' all of the work. Good thing that one worked out, huh?"

"So, you sort of *hitchhiked!*" Mateo said grinning.

"It ain't hitchhikin', Matty-boy, when ya *know* the driver. And don't you go thinkin' about doin' anything like that. Ever!" It was quite amusing, Mateo thought, to hear a motherly tone coming out of your dog. "Anyway, we just felt you kids'd do better if ya didn't know we was around. Besides, Margie likes to play things low key, and even though I'm the means of transportation, she's still throwin' her weight around in the ole noggin."

Mateo grinned and leaned forward eagerly. "Okay, Teach. Don't leave us in suspense! What happened to Broogue?"

Mrs. Morph rolled over and sat up on her haunches. "Let's just say he ain't gonna be a problem anymore, Matty. Y'see, when I jumped on top of him, it was the first time the four of us had been in direct contact again since the day he stole some of our powers with his mental hocus pocus. Well, my takin' him down really shook him up. Then, there's the Doc and Margie along for the ride—which he didn't suspect until it was too late!"

"I was able to facilitate a merger between them for a few moments," Dirk explained, "but then I lost consciousness."

"We didn't know what would happen," Mrs. Morph continued the explanation as she walked on both hind legs and gestured with her front paws to demonstrate her excitement. "But when we came together again somethin' wild started shakin' inside. The abilities Marcus stole from us came flyin' outta him—I felt the pull of 'em leavin' and him tryin' ta hang on, but I tell ya I don't know where they went!"

Dirk smiled and pointed to his chest with both hands. "I . . . um . . . I'm not sure why, but I'm the guy who got them. I think, maybe, because I was facilitating the merger, and you were no longer in three separate physical bodies, your powers just flowed into me."

The collie paused a moment and tilted her head slightly as if listening to some sound that no one else could hear. Then, "Yes, I heard ya, Margie. Yes, I'll tell 'em, Margie!" The collie shook her coat as if she were throwing off loose water. "Margie's explanation is, and I quote, 'history has a way of righting itself—sometimes without our understanding—but always at the appropriate *time!*' Myself—I don't go around sayin' big fancy-pants stuff like that. I just say what's meant to be is meant to be, and you, kid, are supposed to have the powers Marcus stole from us." The collie lay at Mateo's feet now and rested her head on her front paws. "I can't change shape no more! Nope, there just ain't enough juice left in the ol' coffee pot, as Pop used to say."

Mateo chuckled, "Teach, why would there be juice in a coffee . . ."

"WOOF!" Mrs. Morph's bark was shrill. "Matty, don't go questionin' Pop's wise sayin's; God rest his soul—the man was one a them genius-types that was never truly appreciated. Anyway, the pointa all this is that Marcus ain't up to no good anymore." The collie cracked a piece of chewing gum. "And the *best* part, I mean what really thrills this girl in particular, is that without Margie's ability to do one a them time whizbangers, he's stuck there in the past! Gotta love it. I'm bettin' he applies for your old job, kid." She looked at Dirk, who screwed up his face quizzically. "You know— doin' repairs on that old apartment building. Whatdaya bet he ends up in trouble with *the super!*"

A chorus of laughter erupted from all of them, and the collie thumped her tail hard against the ground. "Ya know, Matty-boy, that Lassie was a pretty loyal dog. She was a tough old broad, too, that Lassie. She was a lot like yours truly—nobody messed with her much, if ya know what I mean."

Keiko looked at the collie and asked the question she knew Dirk and the others had been avoiding. "Mrs. Morph, if the Merger is gone, so much will be different. Will Lisa be alive? What about our parents?"

The collie cocked her head; she appeared to be listening again—most likely to Madam. "Listen, sweetcakes," Mrs. Morph confided, "I got it from a very reliable source—a gal who knows a bunch about time—that you're about to walk into a brand new world."

Nicci knew, somehow, what Madam would have said next, and so she spoke the very words Mrs. Morph was about to recite. "And when something is brand new, the possibilities . . . are endless."

Dirk pulled Keiko to her feet. "Okay, guys! It's time to check out those possibilities. Anybody mind if I lead the way?"

"*You* want to lead?" Keiko questioned as she squeezed his hand gently.

"Yeah," Dirk replied, "yeah, I guess I do."

Nicci reached for Mateo's hand but shot him a warning glance at the same time. "Don't get any ideas, Romeo," she said coyly. "I just want you to steady me on the climb down."

He grinned. He wasn't quite sure what to make of her gesture and decided, for right now, to just enjoy it. He reached down and patted the collie's head. "Ya know what, Teach, I think those new possibilities are pretty exciting."

The collie shook herself. "Matty, it's truer than ya can ever know."

And so they made their way to the city below. There was

no cause for worry if they were seen. Should someone wander past them, there would be nothing noteworthy to report, just four kids and their dog spending a lazy afternoon together. The fact that their skin was a different color—one from the other—would be of no consequence, for the same could be said of the vast array of people who populated the city below. And it was true, now, in every town and village spreading out in every direction . . . for as far as the eye could see.